The Catholic Novena Book

by Devin Rose

Contents

Introduction

I had been a single Catholic man for five years, hoping and praying to meet my future wife, but so far it hadn't happened, and I was starting to lose hope.

"Anytime you're ready, Lord, bring us together," I said to God wearily. Sometimes being alone just got really, well, lonely. But God didn't seem to be moving.

I had joined two Catholic singles websites, which at the time most people thought was an act of desperation, and for years had messaged and even met a few Catholic women. But nothing moved beyond friendship. I sent out the word to the elderly

friends of mine who I went to daily Mass with:
"If you have a granddaughter or niece or
friend's daughter who is a faithful Catholic and
who you think would be a good match for me,
introduce us!" And actually they did. I went out
on a date with a very nice young woman,
faithful Catholic. But once again there was
nothing beyond friendship between us.

Finally, I had had it. And I lay down the
challenge to our Lord: "I'm praying the St.
Joseph novena to find my future wife. Don't let
me down." And I started praying the novena,
asking St. Joseph to intercede for me and
speedily bring us together. I gave him four
months to make it happen.

What do you know? A week later I met a young woman, Catherine, via one of the Catholic singles sites I had been on for years. We began corresponding, and hit it off, and then met in person, and after a series of near-disasters we began a courtship, and then were engaged to be married! Just one year from the time I had challenged St. Joseph, Catherine and I were married. How's that for God answering prayer?

Stories of answered prayer encourage us and remind us that God is faithful, in spite of the sufferings we face, disappointments, and difficulties. We have all experienced many times when God seems to not answer or prayers, or He answers them in a way that we don't recognize or like. Oftentimes, in hindsight, we realize that if God had given us what we were asking for, it would not have been the best for us.

Novenas, Past and Present

In this book I am going to share with you the interesting history of novenas in the Catholic Church, stories of real people who have had their novena prayers answered by God, and many novenas themselves.

What Are Novenas?

Novenas enjoy a firm place in the hearts of billions of faithful Catholics, and this unique devotion developed organically in the Church over centuries. It was a grass-roots type of growth, rather than the Church making a decree that "thou shalt pray novenas." Quite the opposite in fact, novenas have only in the relative recent past received any sort of formal recognition in the Church.

Novenas are a private or public prayer where, typically once per day for nine days, a person asks God for a specific request or intention. Usually novenas are directed to God through a particular saint's prayers; hence, the St. Joseph Novena, or the St. Michael Novena, but some novenas are addressed directly to God. (Novena comes from novem, which means nine.)

The very first novena that ever occurred is found in the Scriptures: in the beginning of the book of Acts, just before His ascension to the Father, Jesus gives this direction to the Apostles:

"The former treatise I made, O Theophilus, of all things which Jesus began to do and to teach, until the day on which, giving commandments by the Holy Ghost to the apostles whom he had chosen, he was taken up.

To whom also he shewed himself alive after his passion, by many proofs, for forty days appearing to them, and speaking of the kingdom of God. And eating together with them, he commanded them, that they should

not depart from Jerusalem, but should wait for

the promise of the Father, which you have

heard (saith he) by my mouth.

For John indeed baptized with water, but

you shall be baptized with the Holy Ghost, not

many days hence.

They therefore who were come together,

asked him, saying: Lord, wilt thou at this time

restore again the kingdom to Israel?

But he said to them: It is not for you to

know the times or moments, which the Father

hath put in his own power:

But you shall receive the power of the

Holy Ghost coming upon you, and you shall be

witnesses unto me in Jerusalem, and in all

Judea, and Samaria, and even to the uttermost part of the earth." (Acts 1:1-8)

Nine days later, on the feast of Pentecost, as the Apostles prayed in the Upper Room in Jerusalem, God sent the Holy Spirit upon them. This "novena to the Holy Spirit" thus became the first novena, and the model of all that would come after it.

What's the History of Novenas?

While this first novena occurred at the beginning of the Church's existence, novenas as a nine-day prayer as we know them today arose later on in the Church's history. The first evidence we have of a novena-like prayer is found in the nine days of mourning after someone died, where a "novena of Masses" was offered for their souls, which began at least as early as the fourth century. This custom became enshrined in the medieval period for cardinals and pontiffs.

Alongside these novenas of mourning, in Spain and in France in the 600s arose a novena of preparation before Christmas, where each day symbolized one of the nine months that Jesus was in the womb of the Blessed Virgin Mary. A similar devotion was privately revealed in the 1600s to St. Margaret Mary Alacoque, where He directed her in nine successive first Friday celebrations to honor His nine months in His Mother's womb. Further, in religious communities were seen novenas of

Masses offered in preparation for the feast day

of that community's saintly founder.

The Church in the nineteenth century

gave a formal recognition to novenas when it

attached indulgences to certain ones,

especially novenas in preparation to specific

saints' feast days (e.g. St. Francis Xavier, St.

Joseph). Recall that an indulgence is where the

temporal punishment due for sin is remitted.

These are sins that you are already forgiven of

through Confession, but which have a temporal

punishment associated with them that must be

dealt with (either through indulgences, through

offering of your sufferings to Christ, or in

Purgatory after you die).

Novenas Today

In our own day, we see the flourishing of countless novenas to almost every saint you can think of. The beautiful thing about them is that regular people often have come up with the novena prayers, which over time morph and diverge and combine, so that for any given saint you may find several different novenas, either for different intentions (St. Joseph for fatherhood or for protection or for one's work) or just a unique set of prayers.

(Note that in this book, the novenas that you find I claim no copyright on, even the ones that I have pieced together or come up with portions of. In my view claiming a copyright on a novena is at best counter-productive and at worst at odds with their purpose. And the reality is that most novenas have their origins in old traditions passed down for centuries, so by rights most of the text would be in the public domain anyhow. That said, I have done my best to avoid using any novena text that someone else claims a copyright on.)

How to Pray a Novena

No one dogmatic way exists to pray a novena. However over the course of history in the Church, standard traditional practices have developed.

1. Choose a Novena

You can choose either 1) by finding a novena tailored to your specific prayer request, or 2) by praying a novena on its traditional prayer dates.

For the first option, you can find who the patron saint is for your particular need: St. Jude for impossible or "hopeless" causes, St. Joseph for fatherhood, work, and many other things, St. Anne for a woman to find her future husband, St. Peregrine for cancer sufferers, and so on. Then choose the novena for that saint and begin praying it.

For the second option, you pray a novena that has a traditional date that it is prayed, and offer your intention as the prayer request to God for the novena. For instance, the Divine Mercy Novena takes place beginning Good Friday and ending a week from Easter Sunday (on Divine Mercy Sunday).

St. Joseph's Novena begins in early March and ends on his feast day of March 19th. Other novenas however have no date set for them and can be prayed anytime (Mary Undoer of Knots for instance).

2. Pray Once Per Day with Your Intention

Once per day, pray the novena prayer, asking God for your particular intention.

Usually, a novena will have either one set prayer you pray each day, or it will have a standard introductory or concluding prayer, plus a daily prayer that varies each day.

Missing a day happens to everyone at some point and should not be cause for alarm. Novenas are not superstitious: our Lord hears your prayers and grants the requests through His perfect Wisdom and Love.

3. Meditate on the Prayer

A beneficial practice used by all the saints is to meditate on some truth of the Faith once per day for at least five minutes. Meditation is not magical, and is not Eastern

Mysticism. Instead, you simply raise your heart

and mind to God and contemplate some truth

of Catholicism.

For instance, you could meditate upon

the suffering of Jesus during His Passion

(betrayal, agony in the garden, scourging,

crowning with thorns, carrying His Cross,

Crucifixion). You could meditate on the four

marks of the Church (one, holy, Catholic,

Apostolic), or her three attributes (authority,

infallibility, indefectibility (that she will never

be destroyed or defeated)).

Meditation goes perfectly with novena

prayers because you can meditate on the

prayers of the novena: for example on the

goodness of God as manifested by His saints and especially by His Blessed Mother.

You're On Your Way!

Novenas are a wonderful way to grow closer to God in your faith. We are blessed in the Catholic Church to have access to the communion of saints, God's family. We are not alone but can help each other through prayer to God.

Further, because death does not separate us from God in the Mystical Body of Christ (the Church), we can pray for God's mercy on the souls of those who have died, and ask for the prayers of the saints, whom the Church infallibly declares to be with God in Heaven.

How to Use This Book

You can read the book from cover-to-cover, or jump to a novena that you want to pray and start praying it directly. You can also read through all the different stories and reflections found in the book to find encouragement in your own prayer.

Note that some time back I wrote a mobile app to help you pray novenas, called Pray: the Catholic Novena App. You can download it for free on Apple and Android devices here:

https://pray.app.link/praynovenas

I include a special app link for each novena included in this book, so that you can find it in the app should you so choose.

Chapter One: All About the Saints

All about the Saints

Most novenas invoke the prayers of saints. But what are saints; where do they come from, and how are they recognized? Let's dig into it!

What Is a Saint?

The word "saint" has been used in multiple ways over the past two thousand years. In the New Testament, "saints" refers to the early Christians who were following Jesus in His Church.

But saints who died in Christ's friendship did not cease to be saints; rather, they were now saints in Heaven with God! The Church recognized this fact through proper interpretation of the Scriptures under the light of sacred Tradition. The Church is Christ's Mystical Body, and through baptism we are joined to that Body. Death cannot separate us from it, and so in the communion of saints we are all joined to Christ, whether on earth, in the Church Militant, in Purgatory, the Church Suffering, or in Heaven, the Church Triumphant.

So over the centuries the Church began identifying as saints those holy people who died in God's friendship and were assuredly in

Heaven. At first, this practice was more ad hoc than it is now, but in recent times the process to declare someone a saint became formalized.

Where Do Saints Come From?

Saints come from families, like yours or mine. We are all called to become saints, because we are all called to holiness and heroic virtue. By ourselves it is impossible to achieve, but by God's grace it is possible. Not easy, but possible.

Most Catholics who die in God's friendship are never formally declared saints. That doesn't mean they aren't in Heaven-- quite the opposite!--rather the Church simply cannot go through the full process for investigating the life of every Catholic who dies. Instead, typically the person was known for their faithfulness and holy way of life, and after they die, the Bishop of that area comes forward requesting that their cause be initiated so that the Church will begin an exploration into their life to see whether a full investigation into their holiness is warranted. If there is no objection, the cause is opened and the person declared to be Servant of God.

Normally, five years must pass after the person's death before their cause can be opened. This time period can be waived by the Pope and sometimes is, but it is generally a good idea to let the fervor that sometimes accompanies someone's passing to die down, and then with sober, balanced judgment begin the research into their life.

To be recognized as a saint, many hurdles must be overcome, evidence shown, and ultimately, miracles must occur through the person's intercession. Along the way, a person is first declared to be a Servant of God, then Venerable, then Blessed, and finally, a Saint. The latter two steps are known as Beatification and Canonization and require miracles to be confirmed, typically miraculous health recoveries that defy explanation by modern medicine. Once someone is Blessed it is safe to ask for their prayers (called private veneration; the Church has not yet infallibly determined them to be in Heaven, so only their religious community or diocese can offer veneration in the name of the Church). When the Church declares someone to be a saint, that declaration is infallible, protected by God from error, and the universal Church can venerate them.

The local diocese begins the process when the person is Servant of God, collecting testimony and the person's writings for review. This part of the process can take many years and ends with the diocese declaring whether the Servant of God demonstrated heroic virtue or not. If they have, the documentation is sent to the Congregation for the Causes of the Saints for the next step.

The Congregation has a special person called a Relator to summarize the documentation and present it to the theological commission set up by the Congregation, who then votes on whether the Servant of God showed heroic virtue. The episcopal members of the Congregation then vote and that decides whether the cause continues or ends. If it continues, the Pope gets the final decision about whether they are declared to be heroically virtuous or not. If they are, the Servant of God is now raised to the status of Venerable.

To become Blessed, a verified miracle must occur through the person's intercession, and the diocese in which the miracle occurred (which may be different than the one that originated the cause) is responsible for investigating the miracle on scientific and theological grounds. The Congregation once again votes on this miracle and the Holy Father decides yes or no on it. (In the case of martyrdom the miracle is waived and the decision instead rests on whether the Venerable's death was a true martyrdom or not.)

To become a Saint, a second verified miracle must occur, following the same path as the first miracle for ratification. After that miracle has been confirmed by the Pope, the person can be canonized.

More on Saints and Novenas

New saints are canonized every year! Sometimes these persons died only recently, say in the past ten to twenty years (in the recent past, St. Teresa of Calcutta and Pope St. John Paul II are examples of relatively rapid canonizations), but in most cases the person lived several decades ago, even centuries, before they finally reach the level of canonization. And some persons remain as Servant of God, or Venerable, or Blessed, and never progress further. That is not to say they are not in Heaven, no doubt the vast majority if not all are, but only that the Church has not seen the evidence to merit them being

recognized as such at the current time.

Different regions have particular saints

that they venerate (honor) in special ways. In

Mexico and Latin America, for instance, Our

Lady of Guadalupe is enormously popular. Most

countries have patron saints who hailed from

that nation and exhibited heroic virtue that

exemplifies the area.

And speaking of the Virgin Mary, she is

the same woman of course but recognized

under different titles or appearances

(apparitions) depending on the area: Our Lady

of Czestochowa in Poland, the Immaculate

Conception in France, Our Lady of Guadalupe in Mexico, and so on.

Novenas fit perfectly with the whole process of canonization. People will make holy cards with prayers on them and the image of the person whose cause for beatification or canonization they are promoting. In an old book, I found a holy card with a prayer asking for the Beatification of Fr. Damien, who worked with lepers on a small Hawaiian island. Now he's St. Damien of Molokai!

Then, once someone is declared to be a saint, people will write novena prayers and spread them around via holy cards, books, emails, and websites. Anyone can make up a novena or modify one, and sometimes saints themselves before their deaths make up novenas to other saints!

Someone once asked me: "Where do the saints' images come from and why do they all look similar to one another?" He meant especially the *icons* that he has seen that depict saints. Iconography is a particular style of artwork that follows certain rules. A person is said to "write an icon" rather than paint one. And so when you examine them, you will see that the coloring is quite specific, with certain colors representing divinity or humanity, that the position and shape of the saint's (or of Jesus') fingers are symbolic of the Trinity, or His humanity and divinity, and so on. Icons became the dominant imagery for saints in Eastern Christianity, especially following the defeat of the iconoclasts late in the first millennium. It is said that with icons, it is not so much you looking at the saint, but rather that the icon acts as a window through which the saint is looking *at you*!

Entire books could be written (and have been) about the canonization process and iconography, and the fierce battle against the iconoclasts both in the first millennium and then again when the Protestant iconoclasts renewed the attack on images, destroying beautiful statues, paintings, altars, and desecrating churches. However these fascinating topics are beyond the scope of this book, so you are encouraged to study more on

whichever of these subjects interest you.

Chapter Two: St. Thomas Aquinas Novena

St. Thomas Aquinas Novena

Starts: January 19th

Feast day: January 28th

Introduction

Born in Italy in 1225, Thomas was gifted with an unparalleled intellect. He sought to enter the Dominican Order, but his family stopped him for some time by capturing him and holding him in their castle.

During that imprisonment, they sent in a prostitute to tempt him to sin, but he drove her out, and angels came to him and Thomas was given a special grace of not being tempted against purity again in his life (for those interested in growing in purity, search for the Angelic Warfare Confraternity established by the Dominicans through the graces given to St. Thomas with regard to purity.)

Thomas went on to enter the Dominican Order, become a professor and theologian, writing the Summa Theologiae, the greatest work on faith and reason ever made. He is the patron of Catholic colleges and schools and is sought out by students for help in their studies.

Intro Prayer (to be said each day)

Grant me grace, O merciful God, to desire ardently all that is pleasing to Thee, to examine it prudently, to acknowledge it truthfully, and to accomplish it perfectly, for the praise and glory of Thy name.

In particular, please obtain the favor I ask during this novena: (Make you request here)

Grant me, O Lord my God, a mind to know you, a heart to seek you, wisdom to find you, conduct pleasing to you, faithful perseverance in waiting for you, and a hope of finally embracing you.

Amen.

Daily Prayers

Day 1: God Himself is the rule and mode of virtue. Our faith is measured by divine truth, our hope by the greatness of His power and faithful affection, our charity by His goodness. His truth, power and goodness outreach any measure of reason. We can certainly never believe, trust or love God more than, or even as much as, we should. Extravagance is impossible. Here is no virtuous moderation, no measurable mean; the more extreme our activity, the better we are.

Day 2: Even though the natural light of the human mind is inadequate to make known what is revealed by faith, nevertheless what is divinely taught to us by faith cannot be contrary to what we are endowed with by nature. One or the other would have to be false, and since we have both of them from God, he would be the cause of our error, which is impossible.

Day 3: God loves his creatures, and he loves each one the more, the more it shares his own goodness, which is the first and primary object of his love. Therefore he wants the desires of his rational creatures to be fulfilled because they share most perfectly of all creatures the goodness of God. And his will is an accomplisher of things because he is the cause of things by his will. So it belongs to the divine goodness to fulfill the desires of rational creatures which are put to him in prayer.

Day 4: Many cry to the Lord that they may win riches, that they may avoid losses; they cry that their family may be established, they ask for temporal happiness, for worldly dignities; and, lastly, they cry for bodily health, which is the patrimony of the poor. For these and suchlike things many cry to the Lord; hardly one cries for the Lord Himself! How easy it is for a man to desire all manner of things from the Lord and yet not desire the Lord Himself! As though the gift could be sweeter than the Giver!

Day 5: The world tempts us either by attaching us to it in prosperity, or by filling us with fear of adversity. But faith overcomes this in that we believe in a life to come better than this one, and hence we despise the riches of this world and we are not terrified in the face of adversity.

Day 6: Virgin full of goodness, Mother of mercy, I entrust to you my body and my soul, my thoughts and my actions, my life and my death. My Queen, come to my aid and deliver me from the snares of the devil. Obtain for me the grace of loving my Lord Jesus Christ, your Son, with a true and perfect love, and after him, Mary, of loving you with all my heart and above all things. Amen.

Day 7: Fear is such a powerful emotion for humans that when we allow it to take us over, it drives compassion right out of our hearts. We must love them both, those whose opinions we share and those whose opinions we reject, for both have labored in the search for truth, and both have helped us in finding it.

Day 8: To one who has faith, no explanation is necessary. To one without faith, no explanation is possible. We can't have full knowledge all at once. We must start by believing; then afterwards we may be led on to master the evidence for ourselves.

Day 9: Suppose a person entering a house were to feel heat on the porch, and going further, were to feel the heat increasing, the more they penetrated within. Doubtless, such a person would believe there was a fire in the house, even though they did not see the fire that must be causing all this heat. A similar thing will happen to anyone who considers this world in detail: one will observe that all things are arranged according to their degrees of beauty and excellence, and that the nearer they are to God, the more beautiful and better they are.

Concluding Prayer (to be said each day)

Creator of all things, true source of light and wisdom, origin of all being, graciously let a ray of your light penetrate the darkness of my understanding. Take from me the double darkness in which I have been born, an obscurity of sin and ignorance.

Give me a keen understanding, a retentive memory, and the ability to grasp things correctly and fundamentally. Grant me the talent of being exact in my explanations and the ability to express myself with thoroughness and charm.

Point out the beginning, direct the progress, and help in the completion. I ask this through Jesus Christ our Lord. Amen.

Pray this novena using the app:

https://pray.app.link/uXV086aWXz

Chapter Three: St. Josephine Bakhita Novena

St. Josephine Bakhita Novena

Starts: January 31st

Feast day: February 8th

Introduction

St. Josephine Bakhita was born in Sudan in 1869. She was kidnapped and sold into slavery, suffering tremendously in body and soul.

She was eventually bought by an Italian consul and after some years gained her freedom. She put her faith in Christ and was baptized in 1890. She discerned the call to religious life and became a Canossian Daughter of Charity. Her life was marked by joyful, heroic virtue. She died in 1947 and was canonized in 2000.

Intro Prayer (to be said each day)

In You, Lord, I place my hope, I raise my spirit to my God. You are the God of my salvation, every day I hope in You. Do not let me be disappointed! In this novena I humbly ask for (mention request here).

Daily Prayers

Day 1: Heavenly Father, through the intercession of Saint Bakhita, grant us a great trust in You who are our rock and refuge. Grant that, in every circumstance of life, we may abandon ourselves to you like little children in the arms of the Father. Through Christ Our Lord. Amen.

Day 2: Almighty God, through the intercession of Saint Bakhita, grant us an open and free heart; help us to be content with everything and never lose heart, hoping, in everything and for everything, in our 'Paron' (Master). We ask this through Christ Our Lord. Amen.

Day 3: Heavenly Father, through the intercession of Saint Bakhita, grant us a poor and simple heart, like that of Mary and of your Son who became poor for the love of us. Imitating Him, let us place our confidence not in riches, but in your love and embrace. Through Christ Our Lord. Amen.

Day 4: Almighty God, through the intercession of Saint Bakhita, enwrap us with your meekness and patience so as to enjoy your peace even when things are not as we would like them to be. May your powerful hand sustain us and bless us so that we may enter our Heavenly homeland. Through Christ Our Lord. Amen.

Day 5: Heavenly Father, through the intercession of Saint Bakhita, give us always a hunger and thirst for holiness so that everyone may be saved and come to know and love Jesus, the Way, the Truth and the Life. He lives and reigns forever. Amen.

Day 6: Heavenly Father, through the intercession of Saint Bakhita, grant us sentiments of sincere mercy towards everyone. Grant us that we may heartily forgive the offenses that we receive and thus savour the beauty of your forgiveness. Through Christ Our Lord. Amen.

Day 7: Almighty God, through the intercession of Saint Bakhita, grant us a transparent and upright heart able to contemplate your image in every brother and sister that we meet and with whom we live. Through Christ Our Lord. Amen.

Day 8: Heavenly Father, through the intercession of Saint Bakhita, grant that everywhere we may be instruments of your peace and grant this peace to every family and to the whole world. Through Christ Our Lord. Amen.

Day 9: Heavenly Father, through Saint Bakhita's intercession, grant us to embrace lovingly every moment of our lives and to discover your presence close to us in the signs of the Cross. Through Christ Our Lord. Amen.

Concluding Prayer (to be said each day)

St. Josephine Bakhita, you who lived your daily life with joyful faith, pray for us!

Pray this novena using the app: https://pray.app.link/stjosephinebakhitanovena

Chapter Four: Our Lady of Lourdes Novena

Our Lady of Lourdes Novena

Starts: February 2nd

Feast day: February 11th

Introduction

Our Lady appeared to St. Bernadette Soubirous eighteen times in Lourdes, France in 1858, just four years after the Pope had declared the Immaculate Conception to be dogma.

Bernadette was a poor peasant girl, and many in her town disbelieved that the Virgin Mary had actually appeared to her. But Our Lady told Bernadette to dig in the grotto, and when she did a spring of water spilled forth. When people washed in the spring they received miraculous healings unexplainable by doctors.

When Bernadette asked what the Lady's name was, she answered "I am the Immaculate Conception." Bernadette went on to enter the Sisters of Charity of Nevers, suffered a great deal physically, and died at just 35 years old. She was canonized in 1933.

Intro Prayer (to be said each day)

Ever Immaculate Virgin, Mother of Mercy, we call upon you as Health of the Sick, Refuge of Sinners, and Comfort to the Afflicted.

You know my wants, my troubles, my sufferings. Deign to cast upon me a look of mercy. By appearing in the Grotto of Lourdes, you were pleased to make it a sanctuary whence you dispense your favors, and already many sufferers have obtained the cure of their infirmities, both spiritual and physical.

I come, therefore, with the most unbounded confidence to implore your maternal intercession. Obtain, O loving Mother, the granting of my requests (mention them here).

Through gratitude for favors, I will endeavor to imitate your virtues that I may one day share your glory.

Daily Prayers

Day 1: Our Lady of Lourdes, chosen from all eternity to be the Mother of the Eternal Word and in virtue of being the Immaculate Conception, we kneel before you as did young Bernadette at Lourdes and pray with childlike trust in you that as we contemplate your glorious appearance at Lourdes, you will look with mercy on our present petition and secure for us a favorable answer to the request for which we are making this novena.

Day 2: We give you thanks, Almighty God, for sending your Blessed Mother to the Grotto of Lourdes, saying to Saint Bernadette: I am the Immaculate Conception. O Immaculate Mary, inflame our hearts with one ray of the burning love of your pure heart. Let them be consumed with love for Jesus and for you, in order that we may merit one day to enjoy your glorious eternity. O dispenser of His graces here below, take into your keeping and present to your Divine Son the petition for which we are making this novena.

Day 3: O Mary, conceived without sin, pray for us who have recourse to thee. O star of sanctity, as on that day in Lourdes you spoke to Bernadette and a fountain sprung forth from the ground, bringing with it miracles from our Lord. Now I beseech you to hear our fervent prayer and grant us the petition we now so earnestly seek.

Day 4: Queen of Heaven, we your wayward children join our unworthy prayers of praise and thanksgiving to those of the angels and saints and your own. We pray the Holy Trinity may be glorified in heaven and on earth. Our Lady of Lourdes, as you looked down with love and mercy upon Bernadette as she prayed her rosary in the grotto, look down now, we beseech you, with love and mercy upon us. Obtain for us the graces from your Divine Son and dispense them to us in in our needs, in particular for the special favor we seek in this novena.

Day 5: O Mother of God and our mother, from the heights of your dignity look down mercifully upon us while we, full of confidence in your unbounded goodness and confident that your Divine Son will look favorably upon any request you make of Him in our behalf, we beseech you to come to our aid and secure for us the favor we seek in this novena.

Day 6: O Blessed Mother, so powerful under your title of Our Lady of Lourdes, to you we raise our hearts and hands to implore your

powerful intercession in obtaining from the

gracious Heart of Jesus all the helps and

graces necessary for our spiritual and temporal

welfare and for the special favor we so

earnestly seek in this novena.

Day 7: Father in Heaven, who by the

Immaculate Conception of the Blessed Virgin

Mary did prepare a worthy dwelling place for

your Son, we humbly beseech you that as we

contemplate the apparition of Our Lady of

Lourdes, we may be blessed with health of

mind and body. O most gracious Mother Mary,

beloved Mother of Our Redeemer, look with

favor upon us as you did that day on

Bernadette and intercede with Him for us that

the favor we now so earnestly seek may be granted to us.

Day 8: O Mary our Queen, from heaven itself you came to appear to Bernadette in the Grotto of Lourdes! And as Bernadette knelt at your feet and the miraculous spring burst forth, O Mother of God, we kneel before you today to ask that in your mercy you plead with your Divine Son to grant the special favor we seek in this novena.

Day 9: Immaculate Mother of our Lord Jesus Christ, to you we raise our hearts to implore your intercession in obtaining from the benign Heart of Jesus all the graces necessary for our spiritual and temporal welfare, particularly for the grace of a happy death. O Mother of our Divine Lord, as we conclude this novena for the special favor we seek at this time..

Concluding Prayer (to be said each day)

O star of purity, Mary Immaculate, Our Lady of Lourdes, glorious in your assumption, triumphant in your coronation, show unto us the mercy of thy Son. Virgin Mary, Queen and Mother, be our comfort, hope, strength, and consolation. Amen.

Our Lady of Lourdes, pray for us.

Saint Bernadette, pray for us.

Pray this novena using the app:

https://pray.app.link/e6p7RBnKoA

Chapter Five: St. Joseph Novena

St. Joseph Novena

Starts: March 10th

Feast day: March 19th

Introduction

St. Joseph was the husband of the Blessed Virgin Mary and the foster-father to Jesus Christ. He is known for his righteousness, purity, strength, and practical skills. This novena invokes his intercession for any intention that you have.

Intro Prayer (to be said each day)

Saint Joseph, I, your unworthy child, greet you. You are the faithful protector and intercessor of all who love and venerate you. You know that I have special confidence in you and that, after Jesus and Mary, I place all my hope of salvation in you, for you are especially powerful with God and will never abandon your faithful servants.

Therefore I humbly invoke you and commend myself, with all who are dear to me and all that belong to me, to your intercession. I beg of you, by your love for Jesus and Mary, not to abandon me during life and to assist me at the hour of my death.

Glorious Saint Joseph, spouse of the Immaculate Virgin, obtain for me a pure, humble, charitable mind, and perfect resignation to the divine Will. Be my guide, my father, and my model through life that I may merit to die as you did in the arms of Jesus and Mary.

Loving Saint Joseph, faithful follower of Jesus Christ, I raise my heart to you to implore your powerful intercession in obtaining from the Divine Heart of Jesus all the graces necessary for my spiritual and temporal welfare, particularly the grace of a happy death, and the special grace I now implore:

(Mention your request).

Guardian of the Word Incarnate, I feel confident that your prayers on my behalf will be graciously heard before the throne of God. Amen.

Novena Prayers

Day 1: Saint Joseph, I thank God for your privilege of having been chosen by God to be the foster-father of His Divine Son. As a token of your own gratitude to God for this your greatest privilege, obtain for me the grace of a very devoted love for Jesus Christ, my God and my Savior. Help me to serve Him with some of the self-sacrificing love and devotion which you had while on this earth with Him.

Grant that through your intercession with Jesus, your foster-Son, I may reach the degree of holiness God has destined for me, and save my soul.

Day 2: Saint Joseph, I thank God for your privilege of being the virginal husband of Mary. As a token of your own gratitude to God, obtain for me the grace to love Jesus with all my heart, as you did, and love Mary with some of the tenderness and loyalty with which you loved her.

Day 3: Saint Joseph, I thank God for having made you the man specially chosen by Him. As a token of your own gratitude to God, obtain for me the grace to imitate your virtues so that I too may be pleasing to the Heart of God. Help me to give myself entirely to His service and to the accomplishment of His Holy Will, that one day I may reach heaven and be eternally united to God as you are.

Day 4: Saint Joseph, I thank God for your privilege of being God's faithful servant. As a token of your own gratitude to God, obtain for me the grace to be a faithful servant of God as you were. Help me to share, as you did, the perfect obedience of Jesus, who came not to do His Will, but the Will of His Father; to trust in the Providence of God, knowing that if I do His Will, He will provide for all my needs of soul and body; to be calm in my trials and to leave it to our Lord to free me from them when

it pleases Him to do so. And help me to imitate
your generosity, for there can be no greater
reward here on earth than the joy and honor of
being a faithful servant of God.

Day 5: Saint Joseph, I thank God for
your privilege of being the Patron of the
Church. As a token of your own gratitude to
God, obtain for me the grace to live always as
a worthy member of this Church, so that
through it I may save my soul. Bless the
priests, the religious, and the laity of the
Catholic Church, that they may ever grow in
God's love and faithfulness in His service.
Protect the Church from the evils of our day
and from the persecution of her enemies.
Through your powerful intercession may the

church successfully accomplish its mission in this world--the glory of God and the salvation of souls!

Day 6: Saint Joseph, I thank God for your privilege of living in the Holy Family and being its head. As a token of your own gratitude to God, obtain God's blessing upon my own family. Make our home the kingdom of Jesus and Mary--a kingdom of peace, of joy, and love.

Day 7: Saint Joseph, I thank God for your privilege of being able to work side by side with Jesus in the carpenter shop of Nazareth. As a token of your own gratitude to God, obtain for me the grace to respect the dignity of labor and ever to be content with the position in life, however lowly, in which it may please Divine Providence to place me. Teach me to work for God and with God in the spirit of humility and prayer, as you did, so that I may offer my toil in union with the sacrifice of Jesus in the Mass as a reparation for my sins, and gain rich merit for heaven.

Day 8: Saint Joseph, I thank God for your privilege of being able to suffer for Jesus and Mary. As a token of your own gratitude to God, obtain for me the grace to bear my suffering patiently for love of Jesus and Mary. Grant that I may unite the sufferings, works and disappointments of life with the sacrifice of

Jesus in the Mass, and share like you in Mary's spirit of sacrifice.

Day 9: Saint Joseph, I thank God for your privilege of being able to die in the arms of Jesus and Mary. As a token of your own gratitude to God, obtain for me the grace of a happy death. Help me to spend each day in preparation for death. May I, too, accept death in the spirit of resignation to God's Holy Will, and die, as you did, in the arms of Jesus, strengthened by Holy Viaticum, and in the arms of Mary, with her rosary in my hand and her name on my lips!

Concluding Prayer for each day

Remember, most pure spouse of Mary, ever Virgin, my loving protector, Saint Joseph, that no one ever had recourse to your protection or asked for your aid without obtaining relief. Confiding, therefore, in your goodness, I come before you and humbly implore you. Despise not my petitions, foster-father of the Redeemer, but graciously receive them. Amen.

Pray the novena using the Pray Catholic Novena app:

https://pray.app.link/q3UqYnK5qB

Chapter Six: St. Peregrine Novena

St. Peregrine Novena

Starts: April 22nd

Feast day: May 1st

Introduction

St. Peregrine was born in northern Italy around 1260. He grew up in a family in an area that was under interdict from the pope, and when St. Philip Benizi came to reconcile the people back to the Pope, Peregrine attacked him violently.

Some time later, Peregrine repented, found St. Philip and asked his forgiveness, joined the Servite order in Siena, and was ordained a priest. He was renowned for his preaching and holiness. Later in life he developed a cancerous disease in his leg; the doctors planned to amputate it, but after Peregrine prayed fervently the doctors found his leg to be miraculously healed.

As such, Peregrine is the patron of those suffering from cancer and is often turned to for healing from other illnesses.

Intro Prayer (to be said each day)

O good St. Peregrine, patron of those suffering from foot ailments, cancer, and incurable diseases, grant, we beseech you, relief from suffering to (name the names of the persons who are ill).

In your compassion, we beg you to intercede with Our Lord Jesus Christ that mankind may soon find a cure for the dread disease of physical cancer as well as for the moral cancer which grips so much of our world today. Amen.

Daily Novena Prayers

Day 1: O great St. Peregrine, who were yourself converted from a violent and sinful life, grant that those who have strayed from the way of Christ may, like you, be given the grace to repent and amend their ways. Amen. St. Peregrine, pray for us.

Day 2: Good St. Peregrine, who bore the agonies of cancer patiently for so many years, grant us the courage and faith to stand up under our own sickness or weakness. Amen. St. Peregrine, pray for our fortitude.

Day 3: St. Peregrine, as His priest, you dwelt for many years in peace in the House of the Lord. Intercede for us with Him, then, that this troubled world, torn by hatred and violence, may at last know the blessedness of peace with justice. Amen. St. Peregrine, help us bring lasting peace to the world.

Day 4: St. Peregrine, you became a model priest and eloquent preacher. Grant us more vocations in these troubled times. Amen. St. Peregrine, inspire more young men and women to follow in the footsteps of Christ just as you did.

Day 5: O St. Peregrine, just as you were cured from cancer of the body, intercede for us that the cancer of disregard for life may be removed from the world today. Amen. St. Peregrine, pray that the people of the world may heed the teachings of Christ.

Day 6: St. Peregrine, as a youth you led a life of sin. May our Divine Lord grant that your own conversion may inspire our wayward young people today to change their lives as you did and return to Christ. Amen. St. Peregrine, pray for our young people.

Day 7: St. Peregrine, God granted you the grace of a long and fruitful life. Ask Our Lord, Jesus Christ, to lighten the burden of so many of our aged today who are spending their twilight years in pain, sorrow, and loneliness. Amen. St. Peregrine, bring comfort to our aged in their last days.

Day 8: O St. Peregrine, we ask you to heed the anguished cries of those dying from starvation throughout the world today, especially children and old people. Amen. St.

Peregrine, pray that relief may come to those who are suffering from hunger and thirst in body and soul.

Day 9: Finally, O good St. Peregrine, we ask that you intercede for those whom God sees fit to call home. May they die in happiness and peace, confident that they will be with You forever in the presence of Jesus and Mary. Amen. St. Peregrine, pray that we may have strength and comfort in the hour of our death.

Concluding Prayer for each day

Glorious wonder-worker, St. Peregrine, you answered the divine call with a ready spirit, and forsook all the comforts of a life of ease and all the empty honors of the world to dedicate yourself to God in the Order of His holy Mother. You labored manfully for the salvation of souls. In union with Jesus crucified, you endured painful sufferings with such patience as to deserve to be healed miraculously of an incurable cancer in your leg by a touch of His divine Hand. Obtain for me the grace to answer every call of God and to fulfill His will in all the events of life.

Enkindle in my heart a consuming zeal for the salvation of all men. Deliver me from the infirmities that afflict my body, especially (name any ailments you may have).

Obtain for me also a perfect resignation to the sufferings it may please God to send me, so that, imitating our crucified Saviour and His sorrowful Mother, I may merit eternal glory in heaven. Amen.

Pray the novena using the Pray Catholic Novena app:

https://pray.app.link/YC0SSI1QVZ

Chapter Seven: Our Lady of Fatima Novena

Our Lady of Fatima Novena

Starts: May 4th

Feast day: May 13th

Introduction

The Blessed Virgin Mary appeared on 1917 to three Portuguese children: Lucia, Francisco, and Jacinta. From May 13th to October 13th she appeared six times in the little village of Fatima, Portugal.

World War I or The Great War as it was known at the time, was ongoing, leaving devastation across Europe. Our Lady of Fatima came at this pivotal time telling the children that peace was possible if people would heed her warnings.

Lucia, Francisco, and Jacinta were reared in faithful Catholic homes, in a town that remained faithful to the Church amidst persecution from the government. Lucia de Jesus Santos was the youngest of seven children. Her first cousins, Francisco and Jacinta Marto, likewise were devout children from a large family. Through the apparitions of our Lady, the children grew in holiness and wisdom that belied their young age.

Francisco and Jacinta both died a few years later, as our Lady had informed them, while Lucia lived to be 97 years old. Pope Francis canonized Jacinta and Francisco on May 13th, 2017, in Fatima on the 100th anniversary of the apparitions.

The Miracle of the Sun occurred on October 13th, 1917, witnessed by 70,000 people. Our Lady of Fatima had told the children of the date and place it would occur.

All could look directly at the sun without any injury to their eyes. The sun grew in size, shrunk, rotated and spun, looking as if it were dancing. Even non-Catholics and unbelievers witnessed their miracles, and many immediately were converted to God and asked for forgiveness for their sins.

The Church through the local bishop declared the apparitions worthy of belief in October of 1930.

Daily Prayer (say each day for 9 days)

Most Holy Virgin, who deigned to come to Fatima to reveal to the three little shepherds the treasures of graces hidden in the recitation of the Rosary, inspire our hearts with a sincere love of this devotion, so that by meditating on the mysteries of our redemption that are recalled in it, we may gather the fruits and obtain the conversion of sinners, the conversion of Russia and this favor which I so earnestly seek, (mention your request) which I ask of thee in this novena, for the greater Glory of God, for thine own honor and for the good of all people.

Amen.

Then pray three times each:

Our Father,

Hail Mary

Glory Be

Pray the novena using the Pray Catholic Novena app:

https://pray.app.link/C59uI8y5wC

Chapter Eight: St. Rita Novena

St. Rita Novena

Starts: May 13th

Feast day: May 22nd

Introduction

St. Rita of Cascia was an Augustinian nun who lived in the 1300s. She is the patroness of impossible causes, sickness, wounds, marital problems, abuse, and mothers because of her difficult life.

St. Rita was made to marry at the early age of twelve. Her husband was a was cruel man who was physically abusive, yet she met his cruelty with kindness. St. Rita's family was caught up in the internecine strife rampant in Italy at that time. Her husband was killed as a result of the rivalry between the Guelphs and the Ghibellines (which Dante wrote about).

St. Rita received the stigmata from Jesus and died a holy death.

Intro Prayer (to be said each day)

O Holy Patroness of those in need, Saint Rita, whose pleadings before thy Divine Lord are almost irresistible, who for thy lavishness in granting favors hast been called the Advocate of the hopeless and even of the Impossible.

Saint Rita, so humble, so pure, so mortified, so patient and of compassionate love for thy Crucified Jesus that thou couldst obtain from him whatsoever thou askest, on account of which all confidently have recourse to thee, expecting, if not always relief, at least comfort; be propitious to our petition, showing thy power with God on behalf of thy suppliant; be lavish to us, as thou hast been in so many wonderful cases, for the greater glory of God, for the spreading of thine own devotion, and for the consolation of those who trust in thee.

Daily Novena Prayers

Day 1: Glorious St Rita, you wanted to enter the convent but your parents arranged a marriage for you. We pray for those whose hopes have been frustrated. We pray especially for (add your intention). Amen.

Day 2: Glorious St Rita, you lived for many years with a difficult husband at a time when there was no escape. You never stopped praying for him. We pray for all those fleeing from or experiencing domestic violence. We pray especially for (add your intention). Amen.

Day 3: Glorious St Rita, you wanted the best for your sons even if it meant their death. Help all mothers, fathers and guardians of difficult children and teenagers to pray for them, and to entrust them to God's providence and mercy. We pray especially for (add your intention). Amen.

Day 4: Glorious St Rita, you brokered peace between your husband's family and the family of his murderer. We ask you to intercede anywhere in our lives where there is discord and hatred, and for all families affected by animosity. We pray especially for (add your intention). Amen.

Day 5: Glorious St Rita, you did everything God asked of you, but he didn't give you your heart's desire. Help us not to become bitter if God has not rewarded us as we think we deserve. May we humbly ask his will. We pray especially for (add your intention). Amen.

Day 6: Glorious St Rita, you persevered in your desire to enter the convent, waiting on God's time. Eventually, everything became easy and you were able to enter. Help us all to persevere in prayer for our intentions and trustingly accept God's will whatever the outcome. We pray especially for (add your intention). Amen.

Day 7: Glorious St Rita, you endured painful illness and the rejection of your sisters because of the terrible stench of your wound. You accepted this in peace. May we too learn to accept suffering and rejection, knowing God will never reject us. We pray especially for (add your intention). Amen.

Day 8: Glorious St Rita, you were famed for your compassion and wisdom and many people came to ask your help. Intercede for us that we can be open to others. We pray especially for (add your intention). Amen.

Day 9: Glorious St Rita, you are the saint of things despaired of. I pray that you intercede for me in this thing which seems impossible. I promise to use this favour, when granted, to better my life, to proclaim God's mercy, and make you widely known and loved for the glory of God the Father. Amen.

Concluding Prayer for each day

Relying then upon thy merits before the Sacred Heart of Jesus, we pray thee obtain for us our request.

We honor thy perfect union with the Divine Will, thy heroic sufferings during thy married life, the consolation thou didst experience at the conversion of thy husband, the sacrifice of thy children rather than see them grievously offend God, thy miraculous entrance into the convent, thy severe penances and thrice daily bloody scourgings, thy suffering caused by the wound thou didst receive from the thorn of thy Crucified Saviour, thy divine love which consumed thy heart, that remarkable devotion to the Blessed Sacrament on which alone thou didst exist for four years, the happiness with which thou didst part from thy trials to join thy Divine Spouse, the perfect example thou gavest to people of every state of life.

Pray for us, O holy Saint Rita, that we may be made worthy of the promises of Christ. Amen.

Pray the novena using the Pray Catholic Novena app:

https://pray.app.link/stritanovena

Chapter Nine: Novena to the Holy Spirit

Novena to the Holy Spirit

Starts: 10 days before Pentecost

Feast day: on Pentecost

Introduction

The original and oldest novena in the Church.

Jesus Himself instituted this novena when, after His Ascension, he told His Apostles to go to Jerusalem and pray for nine days before receiving the Holy Spirit at Pentecost.

Intro Prayer (to be said each day)

ACT OF CONSECRATION TO THE HOLY SPIRIT: On my knees before the great multitude of heavenly witnesses, I offer myself, soul and body to You, Eternal Spirit of God.

I adore the brightness of Your purity, the unerring keenness of Your justice, and the might of Your love. You are the Strength and Light of my soul. In You I live and move and am.

I desire never to grieve You by unfaithfulness to grace and I pray with all my heart to be kept from the smallest sin against

You. Mercifully guard my every thought and grant that I may always watch for Your light, and listen to Your voice, and follow Your gracious inspirations.

I cling to You and give myself to You and ask You, by Your compassion to watch over me in my weakness.

Holding the pierced Feet of Jesus and looking at His Five Wounds, and trusting in His Precious Blood and adoring His opened Side and stricken Heart, I implore You, Adorable Spirit, Helper of my infirmity, to keep me in Your grace that I may never sin against You.

Give me grace O Holy Spirit, Spirit of the Father and the Son to say to You always and everywhere, 'Speak Lord for Your servant heareth.' Amen.

Daily Novena Prayers

Day 1: Holy Spirit, Lord of Light. From Your clear celestial height, Your pure beaming radiance give. Only one thing is important, eternal salvation. Only one thing, therefore, is to be feared, sin.

Sin is the result of ignorance, weakness, and indifference The Holy Spirit is the Spirit of Light, of Strength, and of Love. With His sevenfold gifts He enlightens the mind, strengthens the will, and inflames the heart with love of God. To ensure our salvation we ought to invoke the Divine Spirit daily, for The Spirit helpeth our infirmity. We know not what we should pray for as we ought. But the Spirit Himself asketh for us.

Almighty and eternal God, Who hast vouchsafed to regenerate us by water and the Holy Spirit, and hast given us forgiveness all sins, vouchsafe to send forth from heaven upon us your sevenfold Spirit, the Spirit of Wisdom and Understanding, the Spirit of Counsel and fortitude, the Spirit of Knowledge and Piety, and fill us with the Spirit of Holy Fear. Amen. Our Father and Hail Mary ONCE. Glory be to the Father SEVEN TIMES.

Day 2: Come, Father of the poor. Come, treasures which endure. Come, Light of all that live. The gift of Fear fills us with a sovereign respect for God, and makes us dread nothing so much as to offend Him by sin.

It is a fear that arises, not from the thought of hell, but from sentiments of reverence and filial submission to our heavenly Father. It is the fear that is the beginning of wisdom, detaching us from worldly pleasures that could in any way separate us from God. They that fear the Lord will prepare their hearts, and in His sight will sanctify their souls.

Come, O blessed Spirit of Holy Fear, penetrate my inmost heart, that I may set you, my Lord and God, before my face forever, help me to shun all things that can offend You, and make me worthy to appear before the pure eyes of Your Divine Majesty in heaven, where You live and reign in the unity of the ever Blessed Trinity, God world without end. Amen. Our Father and Hail Mary ONCE. Glory be to the Father SEVEN TIMES.

Day 3: Thou, of all consolers best, visiting the troubled breast, dost refreshing peace bestow. The gift of Piety begets in our hearts a filial affection for God as our most loving Father.

It inspires us to love and respect for His sake persons and things consecrated to Him, as well as those who are vested with His authority, His Blessed Mother and the Saints, the Church and its visible Head, our parents and superiors, our country and its rulers. He who is filled with the gift of Piety finds the practice of his religion, not a burdensome duty, but a delightful service. Where there is love, there is no labor.

Come, O Blessed Spirit of Piety, possess my heart. Enkindle therein such a love for God, that I may find satisfaction only in His service, and for His sake lovingly submit to all legitimate authority. Amen. Our Father and

Hail Mary ONCE. Glory be to the Father SEVEN TIMES.

Day 4: Thou in toil art comfort sweet, Pleasant coolness in the heat, solace in the midst of woe. By the gift of Fortitude the soul is strengthened against natural fear, and supported to the end in the performance of duty.

Fortitude imparts to the will an impulse and energy which move it to undertake without hesitancy the most arduous tasks, to face dangers, to trample under foot human respect, and to endure without complaint the slow martyrdom of even lifelong tribulation. He that shall persevere unto the end, he shall be saved.

Come, O Blessed Spirit of Fortitude, uphold my soul in time of trouble and adversity, sustain my efforts after holiness, strengthen my weakness, give me courage against all the assaults of my enemies, that I may never be overcome and separated from Thee, my God and greatest Good. Amen. Our Father and Hail Mary ONCE. Glory be to the Father SEVEN TIMES.

Day 5: Light immortal! Light Divine! Visit Thou these hearts of Thine, And our inmost being fill! The gift of Knowledge enables the soul to evaluate created things at their true worth--in their relation to God.

Knowledge unmasks the pretense of creatures, reveals their emptiness, and points out their only true purpose as instruments in the service of God. It shows us the loving care of God even in adversity, and directs us to glorify Him in every circumstance of life. Guided by its light, we put first things first, and prize the friendship of God beyond all else. Knowledge is a fountain of life to him that possesseth it.

Come, O Blessed Spirit of Knowledge, and grant that I may perceive the will of the Father; show me the nothingness of earthly things, that I may realize their vanity and use them only for Thy glory and my own salvation, looking ever beyond them to Thee, and Thy eternal rewards. Amen. Our Father and Hail Mary ONCE. Glory be to the Father SEVEN TIMES.

Day 6: If Thou take Thy grace away, nothing pure in man will stay, All his good is turn'd to ill. Understanding, as a gift of the Holy Spirit, helps us to grasp the meaning of the truths of our holy religion BY faith we know them, but by Understanding we learn to appreciate and relish them.

It enables us to penetrate the inner meaning of revealed truths and through them to be quickened to newness of life. Our faith ceases to be sterile and inactive, but inspires a mode of life that bears eloquent testimony to the faith that is in us; we begin to walk worthy of God in all things pleasing, and increasing in the knowledge of God.

Come, O Spirit of Understanding, and enlighten our minds, that we may know and believe all the mysteries of salvation; and may merit at last to see the eternal light in Thy Light; and in the light of glory to have a clear vision of Thee and the Father and the Son. Amen. Our Father and Hail Mary ONCE. Glory be to the Father SEVEN TIMES.

Day 7: Heal our wounds, our strength renews; On our dryness pour Thy dew, Wash the stains of guilt away. The gift of Counsel endows the soul with supernatural prudence, enabling it to judge promptly and rightly what must done, especially in difficult circumstances.

Counsel applies the principles furnished by Knowledge and Understanding to the innumerable concrete cases that confront us in the course of our daily duty as parents, teachers, public servants, and Christian citizens. Counsel is supernatural common sense, a priceless treasure in the quest of salvation. Above all these things, pray to the Most High, that He may direct thy way in truth.

Come, O Spirit of Counsel, help and guide me in all my ways, that I may always do Thy holy will. Incline my heart to that which is good; turn it away from all that is evil, and direct me by the straight path of Thy commandments to that goal of eternal life for which I long. Our Father and Hail Mary ONCE. Glory be to the Father SEVEN TIMES.

Day 8: Bend the stubborn heart and will, melt the frozen warm the chill. Guide the steps that go astray! Embodying all the other gifts, as charity embraces all the other virtues, Wisdom is the most perfect of the gifts. Of wisdom it is written all good things came to me with her, and innumerable riches through her hands.

It is the gift of Wisdom that strengthens our faith, fortifies hope, perfects charity, and promotes the practice of virtue in the highest degree. Wisdom enlightens the mind to discern and relish things divine, in the appreciation of which earthly joys lose their savor, whilst the Cross of Christ yields a divine sweetness according to the words of the Saviour: Take up thy cross and follow me, for my yoke is sweet and my burden light.

Come, O Spirit of Wisdom, and reveal to my soul the mysteries of heavenly things, their exceeding greatness, power and beauty. Teach me to love them above and beyond all the passing joys and satisfactions of earth. Help me to attain them and possess them for ever. Amen. Our Father and Hail Mary ONCE. Glory be to the Father SEVEN TIMES.

Day 9: Thou, on those who evermore Thee confess and Thee Adore, in Thy sevenfold gift, Descend; Give Them Comfort when they die; Give them Life with Thee on high; Give them joys which never end. Amen

The gifts of the Holy Spirit perfect the supernatural virtues by enabling us to practice them with greater docility to divine inspiration. As we grow in the knowledge and love of God under the direction of the Holy Spirit, our service becomes more sincere and generous, the practice of virtue more perfect. Such acts of virtue leave the heart filled with joy and consolation and are known as Fruits of the Holy Spirit.

These Fruits in turn render the practice of virtue more attractive and become a powerful incentive for still greater efforts in the service of God, to serve Whom is to reign.

Come, O Divine Spirit, fill my heart with Thy heavenly fruits, Thy charity, joy, peace, patience, benignity, goodness, faith, mildness, and temperance, that I may never weary in the service of God, but by continued faithful submission to Thy inspiration may merit to be united eternally with Thee in the love of the Father and the Son. Amen. Our Father and Hail Mary ONCE. Glory be to the Father SEVEN TIMES.

Concluding Prayer for Each Day

O Lord Jesus Christ Who, before ascending into heaven did promise to send the Holy Spirit to finish Your work in the souls of Your Apostles and Disciples, deign to grant the same Holy Spirit to me that He may perfect in my soul, the work of Your grace and Your love.

Grant me the Spirit of Wisdom that I may despise the perishable things of this world and aspire only after the things that are

eternal, the Spirit of Understanding to
enlighten my mind with the light of Your divine
truth, the Spirit on Counsel that I may ever
choose the surest way of pleasing God and
gaining heaven, the Spirit of Fortitude that I
may bear my cross with You and that I may
overcome with courage all the obstacles that
oppose my salvation, the Spirit of Knowledge
that I may know God and know myself and
grow perfect in the science of the Saints, the
Spirit of Piety that I may find the service of
God sweet and amiable, and the Spirit of Fear
that I may be filled with a loving reverence
towards God and may dread in any way to
displease Him.

Mark me, dear Lord with the sign of Your true disciples, and animate me in all things with Your Spirit. Amen.

Pray the novena using the Pray Catholic Novena app:

https://pray.app.link/holyspiritnovena

Chapter Ten: St. Anthony Novena

St. Anthony Novena

Starts: June 4th

Feast day: June 13th

Introduction

St. Anthony of Padua was a Franciscan friar and priest who lived in the early 1200s. Originally from Lisbon, Portugal, he was a contemporary of St. Francis, who entrusted young Franciscans with priestly vocations to St. Anthony's tutelage.

Intro Prayer (to be said each day)

O wonderful St. Anthony, glorious on account of the fame of your miracles, and through the condescension of Jesus in coming in the form of a little child to rest in your arms, obtain for me of His bounty the grace which I ardently desire from the depths of my heart: (mention request here).

You who were so compassionate toward miserable sinners, regard not the unworthiness of those who pray to you, but the glory of God that it may once again be magnified by the granting of this particular request which I now ask for with persevering earnestness.

Amen

One Our Father, One Hail Mary, and Glory Be to the Father, in honor of Saint Anthony.

Daily Prayer

Day 1: O holy St. Anthony, gentlest of Saints, thy love for God and charity for His creatures made thee worthy while on earth to possess miraculous powers. Miracles waited thy word, which thou wert ever ready to speak for those in trouble or anxiety. Encouraged by this thought, I implore thee to obtain for me the favor I seek in this novena. The answer to my prayer may require a miracle; even so, thou are the Saint of miracles. O gentle and loving Saint Anthony, whose heart was ever full of human sympathy, whisper my petition into the ears of the Infant Jesus, Who loved to be folded in thy arms, and the gratitude of my heart will always be thine.

Day 2: O miracle-working St. Anthony, remember that it never has been heard that thou didst not leave without help or relief anyone who in his need had recourse to thee. Animated now with the most lively confidence, even with full conviction of not being refused, I fly for refuge to thee, O most favored friend of the Infant Jesus. O eloquent preacher of the Divine mercy, despise not my supplications but, bringing them before the throne of God, strengthen them by thine intercession and obtain for me the favor I seek in this novena.

Day 3: O purest St. Anthony, who

through thine Angelic virtue was made worthy

to be caressed by the Divine Child Jesus, to

hold Him in thy arms and press Him to thy

heart. I entreat thee to cast a benevolent

glance upon me. O glorious St. Anthony, born

under the protection of Mary Immaculate, on

the Feast of her Assumption into Heaven, and

consecrated to her and now so powerful an

intercessor in Heaven, I beseech thee to obtain

for me the favor I ask in this novena . . . . O

great wonder-worker, intercede for me that

God may grant my request.

Day 4: I salute and honor thee, O

powerful helper, St. Anthony. The Christian

world confidently turns to thee and

experiences thy tender compassion and powerful assistance in so many necessities and sufferings that I am encouraged in my need to seek thy help in obtaining a favorable answer to my request for the favor I seek in this novena . . . . O holy St. Anthony, I beseech thee, obtain for me the grace that I desire.

Day 5: I salute thee, St. Anthony, lily of purity, ornament and glory of Christianity. I salute thee, great Saint, cherub of wisdom and seraph of Divine love. I rejoice at the favors our Lord has so liberally bestowed upon thee. In humility and confidence I entreat thee to help me, for I know that God has given thee charity and pity, as well as power. I ask thee by the love thou didst feel toward the Infant

Jesus as thou heldest Him in thine arms to tell Him now of the favor I seek through thine intercession in this novena.

Day 6: O glorious St. Anthony, chosen by God to preach His Word, thou didst receive from Him the gift of tongues and the power of working the most extraordinary miracles. O good St. Anthony, pray that I may fulfill the will of God in all things so that I may love Him, with thee, for all eternity. O kind St. Anthony, I beseech thee, obtain for me the grace that I desire, the favor I seek in this novena.

Day 7: O renowned champion of the faith of Christ, most holy St. Anthony, glorious for thy many miracles, obtain for me from the bounty of my Lord and God the grace which I ardently seek in this novena . . . . O holy St. Anthony, ever attentive to those who invoke thee, grant me that aid of thy powerful intercession.

Day 8: O holy St. Anthony, thou hast shown thyself so powerful in thine intercession, so tender and so compassionate towards those who honor thee and invoke thee in suffering and distress. I beseech thee most humbly and earnestly to take me under thy protection in my present necessities and to obtain for me the favor I desire . . . . Recommend my request to the merciful Queen of Heaven, that she may plead my cause with thee before the throne of her Divine Son.

Day 9: Saint Anthony, servant of Mary,
glory of the Church, pray for our Holy Father,
our bishops, our priests, our Religious Orders,
that, through their pious zeal and apostolic
labors, all may be united in faith and give
greater glory to God. St. Anthony, helper of all
who invoke thee, pray for me and intercede for
me before the throne of Almighty God that I be
granted the favor I so earnestly seek in this
novena.

Concluding prayer

May the Divine assistance remain always with
us. And may the souls of the faithful departed,

through the mercy of God, rest in peace.

Amen.

O God, may the votive commemoration
of blessed Anthony, Thy confessor, be a source
of joy to Thy Church, that she may always be
fortified with spiritual assistance, and deserve
to enjoy eternal rewards. Through Christ our
Lord. Amen.

Pray the novena using the Pray Catholic
Novena app:

https://pray.app.link/stanthonynovena

Chapter Eleven: Sacred Heart Novena

.

Sacred Heart Novena

Starts: June 14th

Feast day: June 23rd

Introduction

St. Margaret Mary Alacoque was given this devotion by Jesus to His Sacred Heart. It was also prayed everyday by St. Padre Pio.

Jesus' Sacred Heart burns with love for us and meditating on it deepens our gratitude to Him for giving His life for us on the Cross, as well as inspires us to avoid sin and grow in holiness that we might be less unworthy of the gift of Heaven He offers.

Novena Prayer

O my Jesus, you have said: Truly I say to you, ask and you will receive, seek and you will find, knock and it will be opened to you. Behold I knock, I seek and ask for the grace of: (here name your request) (Our Father, Hail Mary, Glory Be) Sacred Heart of Jesus, I place all my trust in you.

Concluding Prayer for Each Day

O Sacred Heart of Jesus, for whom it is impossible not to have compassion on the afflicted, have pity on us miserable sinners and grant us the grace which we ask of you, through the Sorrowful and Immaculate Heart of Mary, your tender Mother and ours.

Hail, Holy Queen,

Mother of Mercy,

Our life, our sweetness, and our hope,

to thee do we cry, poor banished children of Eve,

to thee do we send up our sighs,

mourning and weeping in this valley of tears.

Turn then, most gracious advocate,

thine eyes of mercy toward us,

and after this, our exile,

show unto us the blessed fruit of thy

womb, Jesus.

O clement, o loving, o sweet Virgin Mary.

Pray for us, o holy Mother of God,

that we may be made worthy of the

promises of Christ,

Amen.

St. Joseph, foster father of Jesus, pray

for us.

Pray the novena using the Pray Catholic

Novena app:

https://pray.app.link/sacredheartnovena

Chapter Twelve: Our Lady of Perpetual Help Novena

Our Lady of Perpetual Help Novena

Starts: June 18th

Feast day: June 27th

Introduction

A Byzantine icon from the 1400s depicts Our Lady of Perpetual Help, holding the child Jesus tenderly as He looks at the implements of His Passion. The icon was thought lost with the destruction of the church it was housed in by the French Revolutionaries during their occupation of Rome, but the Augustinians had rescued it and it eventually came under the guardianship of the Redemptorists. Join millions of Catholics who have called upon Our Lady of Perpetual Help in their great needs.

Novena Prayer

Oh Mother of Perpetual Help, grant that I may ever invoke your powerful name, the protection of the living and the salvation of the dying. Purest Mary, let your name henceforth be ever on my lips. Delay not, Blessed Lady, to rescue me whenever I call on you. In my temptations, in my needs, I will never cease to call on you, ever repeating your sacred name, Mary, Mary.

What a consolation, what sweetness, what confidence fills my soul when I utter your sacred name or even only think of you! I thank the Lord for having given you so sweet, so powerful, so lovely a name. But I will not be content with merely uttering your name. Let my love for you prompt me ever to hail you Mother of Perpetual Help. Mother of Perpetual Help, pray for me and grant me the favor I confidently ask of you (mention request here).

Concluding Prayer

Hail Mary three times

Pray the novena using the Pray Catholic Novena app:

https://pray.app.link/ourladyofperpetualhelpno vena

Chapter Thirteen: St. Maria Goretti Novena

St. Maria Goretti Novena

Starts: June 28th

Feast day: July 6th

Introduction

Maria Goretti was born on October 16, 1890 in Italy. By the time Maria was five, her family had become so poor that they were forced to give up their farm, move, and work for other farmers, where they lived in a house that they shared with another family (the Serenellis).

On July 5, 1902, eleven-year-old Maria was sitting on the outside steps of her home, while a young man named Alessandro was close by. Knowing she would be alone, he returned to the house and threatened her with a knife if she did not do what he said; he was intending to rape her. She would not submit, however, protesting that what he wanted to do was a mortal sin and warning him that he would go to Hell. She fought desperately, and he stabbed her numerous times.

The following day, Maria forgave Alessandro and said that she wanted to have him in Heaven with her, then she died of her injuries.

Alessandro was captured and sentenced to 30 years in prison. A bishop, Monsignor Giovanni Blandini, visited him in jail. He wrote a thank you note to the Bishop asking for his prayers and telling him about a dream, "in which Maria gave him lilies, which burned immediately in his hands."

After his release, Alessandro visited Maria's mother and begged her forgiveness. She forgave him, saying that if Maria had forgiven him on her death bed then she could not do less, and they attended Mass together the next day, receiving Holy Communion side by side.

He reportedly prayed to her every day and referred to her as "my little saint." He attended her canonization in 1950.

Alessandro later became a lay brother of the Order of Friars Minor Capuchin, living in a monastery and working as its receptionist and gardener until he died peacefully in 1970 at age 87.

St. Maria Goretti is the patron saint of chastity, rape victims, girls, youth, teenage girls, poverty, purity and forgiveness.

Intro Prayer (to be said each day)

Saint Mary Goretti who, strengthened by God's grace, did not hesitate, even at a young age, to shed your blood and sacrifice life itself to defend your virginal purity, look graciously on the unhappy human race, which has strayed far from the path of eternal salvation. Teach us all, and especially youth, with what courage and promptitude we should flee for the love of Jesus, anything that could offend Him or stain our souls with sin.

Obtain for us from our Lord victory in temptation, comfort in the sorrows of life, and the grace which we earnestly beg of Thee, (Mention your intention here) and may we one day enjoy with Thee the imperishable glory of heaven.

Amen.

Daily Novena Prayers

Day 1: Most lovable little Saint, who valued your purity above any earthly gain, and who sealed this choice with a martyr's death, obtain for me also a strong love of this virtue, so consoling to the Sacred Heart of Jesus and the Immaculate Heart of Mary.

The pleasures of the world create many temptations for me. I turn to your powerful intercession in Heaven, so that with this help I may remain ever loyal to God, no matter what the price. In danger inspire me to repeat with you, No, it is a sin!

Day 2: Dear Saint Mary Goretti, model of loving obedience to parents, teach me to imitate your example.

Help me to overcome all selfishness and stubborn pride, draw my parents to Thee, then lead me to accept this authority as the Voice of God in my life. Help them to direct me aright and enable me to obey their every wish.

Day 3: Dear Little Saint Mary! You were ready for the moment of martyrdom because your short life was given over to daily and heroic self-denial. Your great love of the Sacred Hearts made all this possible.

Teach me to love Jesus and His Blessed Mother, so that I too will be inspired to daily self-denial. I am inclined to pamper myself, to gratify my senses, and to excuse myself from all penance. This keeps me from being a true follower of Christ. Help me, lovable Little Martyr, to a sincere practice of self-denial, so that I may be your worthy follower and thus gain Heaven for all Eternity.

Day 4: Dear Little Saint! Your days were spent in the filth of the marshes, willingly helping your desperately poor parents and family. Obtain for me the grace to accept my present circumstances in life, no matter how difficult or humiliating they may be.

Just one little drop of water, was the only request that fell from your parched lips during those last horrible hours of life. How much I demand, how unhappy I am when I cannot have my share of the world's conveniences and gaudy attractions! Teach me by your heroic example to be content with what I have, to be grateful for the blessings God has already showered upon me.

Day 5: Dear Little Saint, I depend a great deal upon the help of my friends in time of trouble or sorrow. I look for their approval in many things I do. I am disconsolate and lonely when they desert me.

Through your powerful intercession in Heaven, obtain for me the grace to place all my confidence in God. Only by walking constantly in His presence and depending upon His help, will I have the courage to stand up for His laws, even though it may mean loss of friends, criticism and complete removal of worldly comfort. Help me to look for all of my strength in Him.

Day 6: Dear Little Saint! Help me to greater love of my Faith. I have many God-given opportunities to study it but, sad to say, I neglect them. I am even critical of the Priests, Brothers and Sisters who offer their lives that I may better know and love my holy religion.

Dear Saint Mary Goretti, teach me to be thankful for these grace which you did not have. Make me proud of my Faith and ready to die for it, if God should require that of me.

Day 7: Dear Little Saint, never was Jesus more welcome in a human heart than in yours. The Great Day of First Communion could not come quickly enough. In borrowed clothes and head crowned with flowers of the field, you knelt to receive Him into your soul, so rich with Innocence and Love, and this after months of keen anticipation!

O Powerful Intercessor with the Lamb of God, inflame my soul with your ardent longing to receive Jesus in the Eucharist. Obtain for me the grace to put aside laziness and indifference, so that I may often, even daily, allow myself to be consumed in the burning Furnace of Charity. Teach me what true Love really is!

Day 8: Dear Little Martyr! To the last you followed your beloved Jesus. He, while hanging upon His Cross of Suffering, uttered through parched lips, Father, forgive them for they know not what they do. And you upon your bed of pain, burning with fever, forgave your murderer with the words, I too, pardon him... I too, wish him to join me in Paradise.

Grant me the grace, O Heroic Saint, to be charitable to others. Much of my time is spent on vengeful thoughts, seeking how I may pay back to others the harm they have done to me. Teach me to forgive, so that I may not only gain Heaven, but also lead others there who might otherwise be doomed to Hell. If I am to follow Christ, help me to imitate His Charity, even as you have done.

Day 9: Dear Saint Mary Goretti, once again I turn to you, and beg of you in the words of Our Holy Father, Pope Pius XII, that serenity of spirit and deep joy which is the heritage of those who are pure of heart.

Help me to turn to Our Blessed Lady, confident in the hope that she will take my hand as she did yours, and lead me on to Paradise, my heavenly country, there to enjoy with you and Her, the company of God the Father, Son and Holy Ghost for all Eternity.

Concluding Prayer for Each Day

Pray the Litany of the Blessed Virgin Mary:

Lord, have mercy on us

Christ, have mercy on us

Lord, have mercy on us

Christ, hear us

Christ, graciously hear us

God the Father of heaven,

have mercy on us.

God the Son, Redeemer of the World,

have mercy on us.

God the Holy Spirit,

have mercy on us.

Holy Trinity, one God,

have mercy on us.

Holy Mary,

pray for us.

Holy Mother of God,

pray for us.

Holy Virgin of virgins,

pray for us.

Mother of Christ,

pray for us.

Mother of Divine Grace,

pray for us.

Mother most pure,

pray for us.

Mother most chaste,

pray for us.

Mother inviolate,

pray for us.

Mother undefiled,

pray for us.

Mother most amiable,

pray for us.

Mother most admirable,

pray for us.

Mother of good counsel,

pray for us.

Mother of our Creator,

pray for us.

Mother of our Saviour,

pray for us.

Virgin most prudent,

pray for us.

Virgin most venerable,

pray for us.

Virgin most renowned,

pray for us.

Virgin most powerful,

pray for us.

Virgin most merciful,

pray for us.

Virgin most faithful,

pray for us.

Mirror of justice,

pray for us.

Seat of wisdom,

pray for us.

Cause of our joy,

pray for us.

Spiritual vessel,

pray for us.

Vessel of honour,

pray for us.

Singular vessel of devotion,

pray for us.

Mystical rose,

pray for us.

Tower of David,

pray for us.

Tower of ivory,

pray for us.

House of gold,

pray for us.

Ark of the covenant,

pray for us.

Gate of heaven,

pray for us.

Morning star,

pray for us.

Health of the sick,

pray for us.

Refuge of sinners,

pray for us.

Comforter of the afflicted,

pray for us.

Help of Christians,

pray for us.

Queen of Angels,

pray for us.

Queen of Patriarchs,

pray for us.

Queen of Prophets,

pray for us.

Queen of Apostles,

pray for us.

Queen of Martyrs,

pray for us.

Queen of Confessors,

pray for us.

Queen of Virgins,

pray for us.

Queen of all Saints,

pray for us.

Queen conceived without original sin,

pray for us.

Queen assumed into heaven,

pray for us.

Queen of the most holy Rosary,

pray for us.

Queen of Peace,

pray for us.

Lamb of God, who takes away the sins of the world,

spare us, O Lord.

Lamb of God, who takes away the sins of the world,

graciously hear us, O Lord.

Lamb of God, who takes away the sins of the world,

have mercy on us.

Grant we beseech Thee, O Lord God,

that we, Thy servants,

may enjoy perpetual health of mind and body:

and, by the glorious intercession of the blessed Mary, ever Virgin,

be delivered from present sorrow and enjoy eternal gladness.

Through Christ, our Lord.

Amen.

Pray the novena using the Pray Catholic Novena app:

https://pray.app.link/stmariagorettinovena

Chapter Fourteen: St Anne Novena

St Anne Novena

Starts: July 17th

Feast day: July 26th

Introduction

St. Anne is the mother of Our Lady, and as such has been accorded great honor within Catholic Tradition.

She was the spouse of St. Joachim and is invoked in particular for the intention of finding one's future husband. She is also considered the patroness of housewives, women in labor, and grandmothers.

When we consider how virtuous and holy our Blessed Mother was, we can imagine the tremendous graces that our Lord gave to her parents, Sts. Joachim and Anne, that they would faithfully instruct their daughter in the ways of God.

Daily Prayer

Heavily laden with the weight of my troubles, I kneel at your feet and humbly beg you to take my present need under your special protection. (mention your request).

Vouchsafe to recommend it to your daughter, the Blessed Virgin Mary, and lay it before the throne of Jesus. Cease not to intercede for me until my request is granted. Above all, obtain for me the grace to one day meet God face to face, and with you and Mary and all the angels and saints praising Him through all eternity. Amen.

Concluding Prayer

(Our Father)

(Hail Mary)

(Glory be to the Father)

Pray for us, Saint Anne. That we may be made worthy of the promises of Christ.

O Jesus, Holy Mary, St. Anne, help me now and at the hour of my death. Good St. Anne, intercede for me.

Pray the novena using the Pray Catholic Novena app:

https://pray.app.link/stannenovena

Chapter Fifteen: St. John Vianney Novena

St. John Vianney Novena

Starts: July 26th

Feast day: August 4th

Introduction

John Vianney was born in 1786 near Lyons, France. It was just a few years prior to the French Revolution and the execution of countless priests, nuns, religious, and faithful Catholics.

But the evil events of the French Revolution and Reign of Terror only strengthened Vianney's faith, and upon reception of his first Communion he heard

God's call to the priesthood. In 1815, he was

ordained a priest, and he marched to the small

town of Ars, to be the priest.

They townspeople had never seen

anything like Fr. Vianney. He prayed

constantly; he adored our Lord day and night

and reverently said Mass.

He talked of Jesus to them, and of

Heaven and Hell. He preached the Gospel with

power and clarity and the town was moved to

repentance and faith. He continually fasted and

and did penance for the sake of his flock.

His Christlike counsel and love in the

confessional brought people to Ars in droves,

eventually leading hundreds of thousands each

year to make a pilgrimage there, hoping to

receive renewal and graces from encountering the holy priest.

He died a holy death on August 4th, 1859. He is the patron saint of parish priests.

Intro Prayer (to be said each day)

St. John Vianney, you exemplified what a holy priest of Christ should be. Your patience and fortitude in the confessional demonstrated the mercy of God to the penitents who sought forgiveness for their sins.

Like Christ, you were gracious and merciful, yet also you called your flock to repentance and amendment of life. Help me through your powerful intercession along the path to sanctity that our Lord has prepared for me.

In particular, I ask that you obtain for me the graces of (mention your intention here). Amen.

Daily Novena Prayers

Day 1: God, you raised up humble St. John Vianney to show what one priest can do. Pour out your graces upon my parish priest, and all priests, that they follow the saint's example.

Day 2: Jesus, St. John Vianney was a priest after your own priesthood. Give me the courage to proclaim and live the Gospel boldly, as he did.

Day 3: Lord, St. John Vianney sat in the confessional for hours on end. Help me go to Confession frequently and make good confessions, so that I might overcome my faults and grow in holiness.

Day 4: St. John Vianney, you were gentle with sinners who came to you, seeking the forgiveness of God. Pray that I may be merciful to those who sin against me, and forgive them, remembering how much our Lord has forgiven me of.

Day 5: St. John Vianney, you spent hours in prayer, in quiet contemplation, and so were molded into the shape of Jesus Christ. Help me to learn to pray better and spend time in silence with God.

Day 6: St. John Vianney, you prized purity of heart highly and led others to purity. Obtain for me the graces I need to conquer all sins against holy purity and resist temptations against this great virtue.

Day 7: St. John Vianney, you lived for Heaven and the Beatific Vision with the Holy Trinity, encouraging your flock to do the same. Pray for me, that I won't be choked by the cares and worries of this world, but will keep my eyes firmly set on Heaven's unending joy.

Day 8: St. John Vianney, you fervently received Jesus in the Eucharist at each Mass you celebrated. Pray that I am kept free from mortal sin and obtain for me a share in the devotion with which you received Jesus in the Sacrament.

Day 9: Holy priest of Ars, your coming to that town was like a spiritual avalanche in a time of great persecution and darkness. Pray for us that in our dark time, the light of Christ shines forth from us and shows the way to Heaven for all to see.

Concluding Prayer for Each Day

Our Father

Hail Mary

Glory Be

Pray the novena using the Pray Catholic Novena app:

https://pray.app.link/stjohnvianneynovena

Chapter Sixteen: Fourteen Holy Helpers Novena

Fourteen Holy Helpers Novena

Starts: July 30th

Feast day: August 8th

Introduction

The Fourteen Holy Helpers were a group of saints invoked with great fervor during the Black Death in Europe from 1346 to 1349.

These great saints individually were patrons and patronesses of various maladies, and each had developed a large and devoted following over the centuries. It was understandable, then, during the Plague that the faithful turned to their intercession before the throne of God.

While this feast was removed from the Roman calendar in 1969, the fourteen holy helpers remain saints of the Church, even if for some the historical evidence of their lives is scant.

The Holy Helpers are:

St. Achatius: May 8th -- Headaches

St. Barbara: Dec. 4th -- Fever -- Sudden death

St. Blaise: Feb. 3rd -- Ills of the throat

St. Catherine of Alexandria: Nov. 25th -- Sudden death

St. Christopher: July 25th -- Plagues -- Sudden death

St. Cyriacus: Aug. 8th -- Temptations

St. Denis: Oct. 9th -- Headaches

St. Erasmus (Elmo): June 2nd --
Abdominal maladies

St. Eustachius (Eustace): Sep. 20th --
Family trouble

St. George: Apr. 23rd -- Protection of
domestic animals

St. Giles (Aegidius): Sep.1st -- Plagues -
- Good Confession

St. Margaret of Antioch: July 20th -- Safe
childbirth

St. Pantaleone: July 27th -- Physicians

St. Vitus (St. Guy):June 15th -- Epilepsy

Novena Prayer (pray each day)

O Fourteen Holy Helpers, select friends of God, I honor thee as mighty intercessors, and come with filial confidence to thee in my needs, for the relief of which I have undertaken to make in this novena.

Help me by thy intercession to placate God's divine and just wrath, which I have provoked by my many sins, and aid me in amending my life and doing penance.

Because you persevered till death, you gained the crown of eternal life.

Remember the dangers that surround us in this vale of tears, and intercede for us in all our needs and adversities.

(Mention your intention here)

Great princes of heaven, Holy Helpers, who sacrificed to God all your earthly possessions, wealth, preferment, and even life, and who now are crowned in heaven in the secure enjoyment of eternal bliss and glory, have compassion on me, a poor sinner in this vale of tears, and obtain for me from God, for Whom you gave up all things and Who loves you as His servants, the strength to bear patiently all the trials of this life, to overcome all temptations, and to persevere in God's service to the end, that one day I too may be received into your company, to praise and glorify Him, the supreme Lord, Whose beatific vision you enjoy, and Whom you praise and glorify forever. Amen

Pray the novena using the Pray Catholic Novena app:

https://pray.app.link/fourteenholyhelpersnove

na

Chapter Seventeen: St. Philomena Novena

St. Philomena Novena

Starts: August 2nd

Feast day: August 11th

Introduction

Tradition holds that St. Philomena was a Greek princess who became a virgin martyr at 13 years of age.

In 1802 at the Catacombs of Priscilla tiles read "Peace be to you, Philomena." An Italian nun, Sister Maria Luisa di Gesu, was given a private revelation about St. Philomena, who told her she was the daughter of a Greek king who converted to Christianity.

The Emperor Diocletian fell in love with Philomena, but she refused to marry him, and so she was tortured and ultimate beheaded.

Devotion for Philomena grew when her bones were exhumed and miracles began to occur. Many saints have had a devotion to St. Philomena, including St. John Vianney.

She is the patron saint of infants and youth.

Intro Prayer (to be said each day)

O faithful Virgin and glorious Martyr, St. Philomena, who works so many miracles on behalf of the poor and sorrowing, have pity on me.

You know the multitude and diversity of my needs. Behold me at your feet, full of misery, but full of hope. I entreat your charity, O great saint! Graciously hear me and obtain from God a favorable answer to the request which I now humbly lay before you (here mention your petitions.)

I am firmly convinced that through your merits, through the scorn, the sufferings and the death you endured, united to the merits of the Passion and death of Jesus, your Spouse, I shall obtain what I ask of you, and in the joy of my heart I will bless God, who is admirable in his Saints. Amen.

(From the "Novena to St. Philomena" by the Society of St. Paul)

Daily Prayers

Day 1: Illustrious Virgin and Martyr, St. Philomena, behold me prostrate before the throne whereupon it has pleased the Most Holy Trinity to place you. Full of confidence in your protection, I entreat you to intercede for me with God, from the heights of Heaven deign to cast a glance upon your humble client! Spouse of Christ, sustain me in suffering, fortify me in temptation, protect me in the dangers surrounding me, and obtain for me the graces necessary to me. Above all, assist me at the hour of my death. St. Philomena, powerful with God, pray for us. Amen.

Day 2: O great St. Philomena, glorious Virgin and Martyr, wonder-worker of our age, obtain for me purity of body and soul, purity of heart and desire, purity of thought and affection. Through your patience under multiplied sufferings, obtain for me a submissive acceptance of all the afflictions it may please God to send me and as you did miraculously escape unhurt from the waters of the Tiber, into which you were cast by order of your persecutor, so may I pass through the waters of tribulation without detriment to my soul. Amen.

Day 3: O pure Virgin and holy Martyr, cast a look of pity from Heaven on your devoted servant, comfort me in affliction, assist me in danger, above all come to my aid in the hour of death. Watch over the interests of the Church of God, pray for its exaltation and prosperity, the extension of the faith, for the Pope, for the clergy, for the perseverance of the just, the conversion of sinners, and the relief of the souls in purgatory, especially those dear to me. O great saint, whose triumph we celebrate on earth, intercede for me, that I may one day behold the crown of glory bestowed on you in Heaven, and eternally praise him who so liberally rewards for all eternity the sufferings endured for his love during this short life. Amen.

Day 4: O St. Philomena, Virgin and Martyr, whom God glorifies by so many miracles, whom the Vicar of Jesus Christ has named the Protectress of the living rosary and the children of Mary, manifest, more and more plainly from the heights of Heaven, that a voice holy as yours cannot be denied and that we have the right to rely upon your aid. Obtain for us the grace to be faithful to Jesus Christ, even to death. You became known by your miracles. May you intercede for me before the throne of God. Amen.

Day 5: O Virgin and Martyr, St. Philomena, you made a vow of virginity and you stood by it till death offering your life to

Jesus. Your purity was your perfection. I pray to you to help me in my struggle to be chaste and pure. This is a difficult thing to do now, with the influence of the media that tell us that sex, even outside of marriage, is good and recommendable. May your example inspire me and the young people especially to regard their bodies as temples of the Holy Spirit. May I learn to clothe myself modestly and simply so that I may lead people to live this virtue. Amen.

Day 6: O Virgin and Martyr, St. Philomena, you were patient in your endurance to all the sufferings and sacrifices. You did so because you viewed that all the glories of this world are pure vanity. You were not attached

to anything or anyone. You have your eyes
always set on eternity. Help us to live this
virtue of detachment so that we may be ready
to do anything that Jesus asks of us. Help us
put distance to the happiness and successes of
this life so that we may also learn to look
forward to the happiness of heaven. We ask
you, dear saint, to help us develop a heart that
is attached only to God. Amen

Day 7: O St. Philomena, you received
help from Jesus and special grace of
perseverance when you were tortured and put
to death. That special grace was the gift of
courage. Your bold declaration to die for your
faith is a proof that God will not abandon his
children. At times, I doubt God's place in my

own life; in times of difficulties, I easily complain of his absence. Make me understand that God takes care of me, anticipates my needs and protects me from danger. Help me to trust God and put myself entirely in his hands. Amen

Day 8: O dear St. Philomena, you lived during the most terrible time of the Church, when Christians were hunted like animals. But like the first Christians, you found solace being with your brothers and sisters with whom you broke bread, sharing in the Eucharist in the catacombs. You received the Body and Blood of Jesus with devotion, knowing that he alone would be able to help you weather the persecutions. I implore you, my dear saint, to help me love the Eucharist, to receive Jesus daily through the Holy Communion. Bless also my brothers and sisters, especially the sick, who are unable to receive Jesus daily. May Jesus' presence enable them to accept the sufferings they are passing through. Amen

Day 9: O dear St. Philomena, you encountered Christians who, due to terrible tortures, were unable to remain strong and renounce their faith temporarily, or who faced with physical pain, surrendered holy books to the Roman soldiers. You welcomed these Christians and understand their weaknesses. You did not condemn them nor stay away from them. You continued to pray for them and with them. I pray, my dear saint, that you will also help me develop the spirit of understanding

that will prevent me from condemning people.

Inspire me always to work for unity and peace

in our communities especially in our parishes.

Amen.

Concluding Prayer

Saint Philomena, Pray for us!

Pray the novena using the Pray Catholic

Novena app:

https://pray.app.link/stphilomenanovena

Chapter Eighteen: St. Clare Novena

St. Clare Novena

Starts: August 2nd

Feast day: August 11th

Introduction

St. Clare grew up in Assisi and from early in her life was devoted to Christ and His Church.

She heard St. Francis preach and knew that God was leading her to follow him. St. Francis recognized Clare's virtue and set her on a path to ultimately found what we know today as the Poor Clares. Before her death, St.

Clare wrote the Rule for her nuns to follow, and the pope confirmed it.

Intro Prayer (to be said each day)

O most Holy Trinity, Father, Son and Holy Spirit, we praise Thy Holy Name and the wonders of grace Thou hast worked in Thy servant, Saint Clare.

Through her powerful intercession grant us the favors we beg in this novena, above all the grace to live and die as she did in Thy most Holy Love. Amen.

Daily Novena Prayers

Day 1: O Seraphic Saint Clare, first disciple of the Poor Man of Assisi, who hast abandoned all riches and honours for a life of sacrifice and of highest poverty, obtain from God for us the grace we ask (mention your intentions here), that of always submitting to the Divine Will and of living confidently in the providence of our Heavenly Father. Amen.

Day 2: O Seraphic Saint Clare who, notwithstanding living separated from the world hast not forgotten the poor and the afflicted, but hast become a mother to them, sacrificing for them your riches and working for them innumerable miracles; obtain from God for us the grace we implore (mention your intentions here), Christian charity towards our brethren in all their spiritual and temporal

needs. Amen.

Day 3: O Seraphic Saint Clare, light of

your country, who hast delivered Italy from

barbarous invaders; obtain from God for us the

grace we implore (mention your intentions

here), that of overcoming all attacks of the

world against faith and morals thus preserving

in our families true Christian peace with a holy

fear of God and a devotion to the Blessed

Sacrament. Amen.

Day 4: Blessed Saint Clare, whose very

name means light, illumine the darkness of our

minds and hearts so that we might see what

God wishes us to do and perform it with a

willing and joyful heart. Before your birth, a Heavenly voice foretold that you would be a light illuminating the world. Be a light to us in the sorrows and anxieties of this earthly life, and lead us into the eternal light of our home in Heaven. Amen.

Day 5: O Seraphic Saint Clare, whose virginal heart was great enough to love the whole world, take our petitions into your pure hands and present them to God. Pray for us that we may one day enter joyously before the throne of God. Let the light of your perfect purity consume the shadows of sin and corruption that darkens the world. Intercede by your innocence for our youth. Safeguard the peace of our homes and the unity of our family. Plead with your chaste love for all in peril. Amen.

Day 6: Generous Saint Clare, who left wealth and pleasure and all earthly goods to become the first spiritual daughter of Saint Francis and to serve God in the cloister, help us to commit our lives to God without limit or measure so that He may live in us and shine forth from us to all whose lives touch ours. You who loved souls so much as to make your life a continual sacrifice for them, obtain for us the graces we now implore and win for us the strength to praise God in suffering as well as in joy. Amen.

Day 7: Faithful Saint Clare, loyal daughter of the Church, friend and confidante of popes, intercede for the holy Church and look graciously from Heaven on our holy Father Pope. Enlighten us to remove from our souls all that hinders the progress of the Church on earth. Grant that we may share your great love for the church of God and spread His kingdom on earth by a holy life. You, who worked miracles in the presence of the pope on earth, obtain for us the graces we need, now that you stand in the presence of the most high God in Heaven. Amen.

Day 8: Valiant Saint Clare, who fearlessly stood alone against the barbarous Saracens, trusting in the Blessed Sacrament as your only

protection, enkindle in us a tender love for
Jesus Christ; help us to live Eucharistic lives.
You who saved your city of Assisi from plunder
and ruin, protect our city and archdiocese,
plead for our beloved country and the suffering
world. A voice from the Sacred Host rewarded
your trust with a promise: 'I will always take
care of you.' Glorious Saint Clare, from your
high place in Heaven, take care of us now in
our earthly needs and guide us by your light to
Heaven. Amen.

Day 9: Gracious Saint Clare, who fulfilled
your womanhood by a life of love in prayer and
penance, help us to fulfill our destiny that we
may one day greet you in Heaven. You who
were consoled at your death by a vision of

Christ band His Mother, obtain for us the grace
that we may die under the special protection of
God and enter into the life and bliss you now
enjoy. Have pity on us who struggle, on us
who mourn, and win for us the favours of God
so that after this life we may come home to
Him who lives and reigns forever and ever.
Amen.

Concluding Prayer for Each Day

V. Pray for us, Saint Clare.

R. That we may be made worthy of the
promises of Christ.

We Pray Thee, Lord, Grant us Thy
servants who celebrate the festival of blessed

Clare Thy Virgin, by her intercession, to be partakers of the joys of heaven and coheirs with Thine only-begotten Son, Who being God, lives and reigns forever and ever. Amen.

Pray the novena using the Pray Catholic Novena app:

https://pray.app.link/stclarenovena

Chapter Nineteen: St. Monica Novena

St. Monica Novena

Starts: August 18th

Feast day: August 27th

Introduction

St. Monica was born in AD 332 in North Africa. She married a pagan man named Patricius, who by all accounts had a violent temper. He was unsympathetic to St. Monica's Catholic faith.

St. Monica's son was St. Augustine, but he rejected Christ and the Church for many years, living a life of sensuality and hedonism.

After long years of St. Monica's prayers, St. Augustine was converted to Christ and became one of the greatest Doctors of the Church.

She is the patroness of wives and abuse victims.

Intro Prayer (to be said each day)

Exemplary Mother of the Great Augustine, you perserveringly pursued your wayward son not with wild threats but with prayerful cries to heaven.

Intercede for all mothers in our day so that they may learn to draw their children to God. Teach them how to remain close to their children, even the prodigal sons and daughters who have sadly gone astray.

Daily Prayers

Day 1: Today we pray for all God's people who have left the Church. May the Holy Spirit open their ears and hearts so they may hear this invitation to come home.

Day 2: Today we pray for those who were baptized Catholic, but were not blessed with families to guide them to spiritual maturity. May the Holy Spirit guide them back to the Catholic Church.

Day 3: Today we pray for those who have been hurt by someone in the Church. May those of us in the Church today be a source of healing.

Day 4: Today we pray for those who reject the Church's God-given teachings. May the Holy Spirit open their hearts and minds to the truth and wisdom of those teachings.

Day 5: Today we pray for those whose sins make them feel unworthy to come to God. May they repent with hope and feel the warm embrace of Our Father's loving forgiveness.

Day 6: Today we pray for all those children who have grown up and, like St. Augustine as a young man, rejected Christ and His Church. May the grace of God and our prayers draw them back to the Church.

Day 7: Today we pray for those who are resisting Your call due to pressures from friends and family members. May the Holy Spirit give them strength in their convictions and may the Holy Spirit fill the hearts of their friends and family with love and support.

Day 8: Today we pray for those who feel abandoned by God. May they come to see God working in their lives, restore their faith in Him, and come home to His Church.

Day 9: Today we pray for those who are ready to come home and just need to be invited. May the Holy Spirit open our hearts and eyes to them that we may be the inviting and welcoming presence they seek.

Concluding Prayer (to be said each day)

Dear St Monica, troubled wife and mother, many sorrows pierced your heart during your lifetime. Yet you never despaired or lost faith. With confidence, persistence and profound faith, you prayed daily for the conversion of your beloved husband, Patricius and your beloved son, Augustine.

Grant me that same fortitude, patience and trust in the Lord. Intercede for me, dear St. Monica, that God may favorably hear my plea for (mention your petition here).

And grant me the grace to accept his will in all things, through Jesus Christ, our Lord, in the unity of the Holy Spirit, one God forever

and ever. Amen.

Pray the novena using the Pray Catholic

Novena app:

https://pray.app.link/stmonicanovena

Chapter Twenty: Our Lady of Sorrows Novena

Our Lady of Sorrows Novena

Starts: September 6th

Feast day: September 15th

Introduction

We call to mind in this novena the sorrows that our Blessed Mother endured during her life. We live in a valley of tears, until we reach our heavenly homeland, and so we ask our Lady to intercede for us.

She suffered greatly and can console us in our sufferings, obtaining for us grace from God. Her seven sorrows were:

1. The Prophecy of Simeon

2. The Flight into Egypt

3. The Loss of the child Jesus in the Temple

4. The Meeting of Mary and Jesus on the Way to Calvary

5. The Crucifixion and Death of Jesus

6. The Piercing of the Side of Jesus and His Descent from the Cross

7. The Burial of Jesus

Intro Prayer (to be said each day)

O sorrowful Mother, I turn to you in total trust. You suffered the sharpest pains in life, watching your Son die upon the Cross, and yet you remained by Him to the end.

Look with favor upon me, a poor sinner, and obtain for me from your Son all the graces I need to endure the sufferings God allows me to face.

Daily Novena Prayers

Day 1: On the Cross her Son was dying.

Mary stood beneath Him crying,

Sharing in His saving cross.

As He hangs, her soul is grieving,

and a sword her heart is cleaving

and she weeps the bitter loss.

O Mother of Sorrows, through thy First Sorrow, the Prophecy of Holy Simeon, intercede for me with the Sacred Heart of Jesus, and grant me the favor I implore (mention request here).

Day 2: O, the sad, afflicted Mother of the Son beyond all others: only Son of God most high. Full of grief, her heart is aching; watching Him, her body, quaking, trembles as her offspring dies.

O Mother of Sorrows, through thy Second Sorrow, the Flight into Egypt, intercede for me with the Sacred Heart of Jesus, and grant me the favor I implore (mention request here).

Day 3: Who would see Christ's mother crying

at the bitter crucifying

without tears of sympathy?

Who could see her depth of feeling--

thoughts of many hearts revealing--

and not share her agony?

O Mother of Sorrows, through thy Third Sorrow, the Loss of the Child Jesus, intercede for me with the Sacred Heart of Jesus, and grant me the favor I implore (mention request here).

Day 4: Pardon for our sins entreating,

She saw Him endure the beating.

All our guilt on Him was cast.

She stood by in contemplation

When her Son, in desolation

Breathed His spirit forth at last.

O Mother of Sorrows, through thy Fourth

Sorrow, meeting thy Jesus on His Way to

Calvary, intercede for me with the Sacred

Heart of Jesus, and grant me the favor I

implore (mention request here).

Day 5: Font of love, O Blessed Mother,

lend me tears to mourn my Brother.

Never let my ardor dim.

Let my heart be burning freely,

Christ my God be pleased to see me

all on fire with love for Him.

O Mother of Sorrows, through thy Fifth

Sorrow, standing beneath thy dying Son on Mt.

Calvary, the Flight into Egypt, intercede for me

with the Sacred Heart of Jesus, and grant me

the favor I implore (mention request here).

Day 6: This I ask, O Holy Mary,

that His wounds I too may carry:

fix them deeply in my heart.

Mine the burden He was bearing;

let me in His pain be sharing;

of His suffering take a part.

O Mother of Sorrows, through thy Sixth Sorrow, thy Jesus is laid in thy Arms, intercede for me with the Sacred Heart of Jesus, and grant me the favor I implore (mention request here).

Day 7: Let me join in your lamenting,

through my life weep unrelenting

tears for Jesus Crucified.

Let me stand and share your weeping,

all the day death's vigil keeping,

glad to stand close by your side.

O Mother of Sorrows, through thy Seventh Sorrow, the Burial of thy Jesus, intercede for me with the Sacred Heart of

Jesus, and grant me the favor I implore

(mention request here).

Day 8: Queen of all the virgin choir,

judge me not when I aspire

your pure tears to emulate.

Let me share in Christ's affliction--

death by bitter crucifixion--

and His wounds commemorate.

We give God thanks for the exaltation of

His holy Cross, and ask dear Mother of Sorrows

that you pray for us (mention request here).

Day 9: Let me taste the pains He offered,

drunk with love for Him who suffered.

May His wounds become my own.

On the day of Christ's returning

may my heart be lit and burning.

Virgin, aid me at His throne.

May His Cross be interceding

and His death my vict'ry pleading.

May He hold me in His grace.

When my flesh by death is taken,

may my soul to glory waken

and in heaven take a place. Amen.

Blessed Mother, on this last day of our novena to you we entrust ourselves to your heart, pierced with love for your Divine Son (mention request here).

Concluding Prayer for each day

The Memorare: Remember, O most gracious Virgin Mary, that never was it known that anyone who fled to your protection, implored your help or sought your intercession, was left unaided. Inspired by this confidence, I fly unto you, O Virgin of Virgins, my Mother. To you do I come, before you I stand, sinful and sorrowful. O Mother of the Word Incarnate, despise not my petitions, but in your clemency, hear and answer me. Amen.

Pray the novena using the Pray Catholic Novena app:

https://pray.app.link/ourladyofsorrowsnovena

Chapter Twenty-One: Padre Pio Novena

Padre Pio Novena

Starts: September 14th

Feast day: September 23rd

Introduction

St. Pio of Pietrelcina, or Padre Pio as he is affectionately known by millions, was a Franciscan priest gifted by God in amazing ways. Born in 1887, he entered the Capuchin Franciscan order as a young man. He faced countless trials and temptations during his life, received the stigmata, had the gift of being able to read souls, and was attacked by the devil.

Intro Prayer (to be said each day)

Dear God, Thou hast generously blessed Thy servant, St. Pio of Pietrelcina, with the gifts of the Spirit. Thou hast marked his body with the five wounds of Christ Crucified, as a powerful witness to the saving Passion and Death of Thy Son.

Endowed with the gift of discernment, St. Pio labored endlessly in the confessional for the salvation of souls. With reverence and intense devotion in the celebration of Mass, he invited countless men and women to a greater union with Jesus Christ in the Sacrament of the Holy Eucharist.

Concluding Prayer

Through the intercession of St. Pio of Pietrelcina, I confidently beseech Thee to grant me the grace of (mention your intentions here).

Amen.

Pray the Glory Be three times.

Pray the novena using the Pray Catholic Novena app: https://pray.app.link/tb2nsnsgtG

Chapter Twenty-Two: St. Raphael Novena

St. Raphael Novena

Starts: September 20th

Feast day: September 29th

Introduction

St. Raphael is one of the Archangels, only three of whom are named in the Scriptures (Sts. Michael and Gabriel are the other two).

His name means God has healed, and he appears only in the book of Tobit in the Bible. (Note that Protestants removed this book and six others from the Scriptures during the

1500s, so your Protestant friends do not believe what Catholics do about St. Raphael.)

In Tobit, St. Raphael reveals himself as the angel Raphael, one of the seven, who stand before the Lord. He is the patron saint of travelers, the blind, and for bodily ills, and he is also invoked for finding one's future spouse.

Some believe that he is also the angel who in John 5 touched the waters of the pool that the infirm waited beside in hopes of healing.

Daily Prayer (say each day)

Glorious Archangel Saint Raphael, great prince of the heavenly court, you are illustrious for your gifts of wisdom and grace.

You are a guide of those who journey by land or sea or air, consoler of the afflicted, and refuge of sinners. I beg you, assist me in all my needs and in all the sufferings of this life, as once you helped the young Tobias on his travels.

Because you are the medicine of God, I humbly pray you to heal the many infirmities of my soul and the ills that afflict my body. I especially ask of you the favor (mention your request here) and the great grace of purity to prepare me to be the temple of the Holy Spirit. Amen.

St. Raphael, of the glorious seven who stand before the throne of Him who lives and reigns, Angel of health, the Lord has filled your hand with balm from heaven to soothe or cure our pains. Heal or cure the victim of disease, and guide our steps when doubtful of our ways.

Pray the novena using the Pray Catholic Novena app:

https://pray.app.link/straphaelnovena

Chapter Twenty-Three: St. Michael the Archangel Novena

St. Michael the Archangel

Novena

Starts: September 20th

Feast day: September 29th

Introduction

St. Michael is one of the Archangels and is mentioned several times in the Bible. He leads the Heavenly Hosts into battle, will fight and defeat Satan in the last days, and he will call men to their Judgment. He is invoked regularly by millions via the St. Michael prayer for protection against evil.

Intro Prayer (to be said each day)

Saint Michael the Archangel, loyal champion of God and His Catholic people, I turn to thee with confidence and seek thy powerful intercession. For the love of God, Who hast made thee so glorious in grace and power, and for the love of the Mother of Jesus, the Queen of the Angels, be pleased to hear my prayer.

Thou knowest the value of my soul in the eyes of God. May no stain of evil ever disfigure its beauty. Help me to conquer the evil spirit who tempts me. I desire to imitate thy loyalty to God and Holy Mother Church and thy great love for God and men. And since thou art God's messenger for the care of His people, I entrust to thee this special request: (Here mention your request.)

Saint Michael, since thou art, by the will of the Creator, the powerful intercessor of Christians, I have great confidence in thy prayers. I earnestly trust that if it is God's holy will, my petition will be granted.

Concluding Prayer for each day

Pray for me, Saint Michael, and also for those I love. Protect us in all dangers of body and soul. Help us in our daily needs. Through thy powerful intercession, may we live a holy life, die a happy death and reach Heaven where we may praise and love God with thee forever. Amen.

Pray the novena using the Pray Catholic Novena app:

https://pray.app.link/stmichaelnovena

Chapter Twenty-Four: St. Therese of Lisieux Novena

St. Therese of Lisieux Novena

Starts: September 22nd

Feast day: October 1st

Introduction

St. Thérèse was a French Discalced Carmelite nun who lived in the late 1800s. She has been a highly influential model of sanctity for Catholics and for others because of the simplicity and practicality of her approach to the spiritual life. Together with Saint Francis of

Assisi, she is one of the most popular saints in the history of the church.

Pope Pius X called her "the greatest saint of modern times" while Pope St. John Paul II named her a Doctor of the Church (only the third female Doctor at that time).

Intro Prayer (to be said each day)

O Little Therese of the Child Jesus, please pick for me a rose from the heavenly garden and send it to me as a message of love.

O Little Flower of Jesus, ask God to grant the favors I now place with confidence in your hands:

(mention your special prayer request here)

St. Therese, help me to always believe as you did, in God's great love for me, so that I may imitate your "Little Way" each day.

Pray the novena using the Pray Catholic Novena app:

https://pray.app.link/stthereseoflisieuxnovena

Chapter Twenty-Five: St. Jude Novena

St. Jude Novena

Starts: October 19th

Feast day: October 28th

Introduction

St. Jude was one of the Apostles of Jesus Christ.

Pray this novena especially for "hopeless" causes, desperate situations, and grave illnesses.

Intro Prayer (to be said each day)

Most holy Apostle, St. Jude, faithful servant and friend of Jesus, the Church honors and invokes you universally, as the patron of difficult cases, of things almost despaired of.

Pray for me, I am so helpless and alone.

Intercede with God for me that He bring visible and speedy help where help is almost despaired of. Come to my assistance in this great need that I may receive the consolation and help of heaven in all my necessities, tribulations, and sufferings, particularly: (make your request here) and that I may praise God with you and all the saints forever. I promise, O Blessed St. Jude, to be ever mindful of this great favor granted me by God and to always honor you as my special and powerful patron, and to gratefully encourage devotion to you.

Amen.

Concluding Prayer for each day

May the Most Sacred Heart of Jesus be adored, and loved in all the tabernacles until the end of time. Amen.

May the most Sacred Heart of Jesus be praised and glorified now and forever. Amen

St. Jude pray for us and hear our prayers. Amen.

Blessed be the Sacred Heart of Jesus

Blessed be the Immaculate Heart of Mary

Blessed be St. Jude Thaddeus, in all the world and for all Eternity.

(Our Father, Hail Mary)

Pray the novena using the Pray Catholic

Novena app:

https://pray.app.link/stjudenovena

Chapter Twenty-Six: Immaculate Conception Novena

Immaculate Conception Novena

Starts: October 19th

Feast day: October 28th

Introduction

From early in the Church's history, saints spoke of the Blessed Virgin Mary with the highest regard, in particular regarding her purity and holiness.

The words of the Archangel Gabriel to her, addressing her as Full of Grace, conveyed a perfection of grace as a past and present state--in a word, a singular grace given to her by God to be preserved from the stain of original sin.

In her wisdom, the Church was careful to preserve this Tradition, and reverence and veneration of Our Lady grew as the centuries passed. Then, in the mid-1800s, the Church declared the Immaculate Conception to be irreformable dogma. A few years later Our Lady appeared to St. Bernadette in Lourdes, France and confirmed that she was "the Immaculate Conception."

Intro Prayer (to be said each day)

Immaculate Virgin Mary, you were pleasing in the sight of God from the first moment of your conception in the womb of your mother, St. Anne. You were chosen to be the mother of Jesus Christ, the Son of God. I believe the teaching of holy Mother the Church, that in the first instant of your conception, by the singular grace and privilege of Almighty God, in virtue of the merits of Jesus Christ, Savior of the human race and beloved Son, you were preserved from all stain of original sin. I thank God for this wonderful privilege and grace he bestowed upon you as I honor your Immaculate Conception.

Look graciously upon me as I implore this special favor: (mention your request).

Virgin Immaculate, Mother of God and my Mother, from your throne in heaven turn your eyes of pity upon me. Filled with confidence in your goodness and power, I beg you to help me in this journey of life which is so full of dangers for my soul. I entrust myself entirely to you, that I may never be the slave of the devil through sin, but may always live a humble and pure life. I consecrate myself to you forever, for my only desire is to love your divine Son Jesus. Mary, since none of your devout servants has perished, May I too be saved.

Concluding Prayer for each day

Hail Mary

Glory Be

Pray the novena using the Pray Catholic

Novena app:

https://pray.app.link/1N4jgcAwVx

Chapter Twenty-Seven: Our Lady of Guadalupe Novena

Our Lady of Guadalupe Novena

Starts: December 3rd

Feast day: December 12th

Introduction

Our Lady appeared in the year 1531 to Juan Diego, a simple peasant of Aztec descent who had converted to Catholicism.

She told him to have the bishop build a church on the hill where she appeared, and Juan Diego dutifully told the bishop, but he was not believed at first; instead, a miraculous

sign was demanded to prove it was Our Lady.

Our Lady worked the miraculous sign by

having roses grow on this hill in the winter,

then arranged the roses in Juan Diego's tilma

(a long tunic), and when Juan Diego showed

the bishop by letting the roses fall to the

ground, not only did the roses themselves

demonstrate the authenticity of the

appearance but even more so the fact that the

roses had miraculously blazed an image of Our

Lady of Guadalupe on his tilma.

The bishop believed him at once and a

church was built on the hill. The mass

conversion of the Aztec people by the millions followed.

The tilma remains intact to this day, almost five hundred years later, another testament to the miraculous nature of it, as the fiber should have decomposed long ago. Juan Diego was later canonized as well as a testament to his holiness.

Intro Prayer (to be said each day)

Remember, O most gracious Virgin of Guadalupe, that in your heavenly apparitions on the mount of Tepeyac, you promised to show your compassion and pity towards all who, loving and trusting you, seek your help and call upon you in their necessities and afflictions. You promised to hear our supplications, to dry our tears, and to give us consolation and relief.

Never has it been known that anyone who fled to your protection, implored your help, or sought your intercession, was left unaided. Inspired by this confidence, we fly to you, O Mary, ever-Virgin Mother of the true God! Though grieving under the weight of our sins, we come to prostrate ourselves before you. We fully trust that, standing beneath your shadow and protection, nothing will trouble or afflict us, nor do we need to fear illness or misfortune, or any other sorrow.

O Virgin of Guadalupe, you want to remain with us through your admirable Image, you who are our Mother, our health, and our life. Placing ourselves beneath your maternal gaze, and having recourse to you in all our necessities, we need do nothing more.

O Holy Mother of God, despise not our petitions, but in your mercy hear and answer us. Amen.

Daily Prayers

Day 1: Dearest Lady of Guadalupe, fruitful Mother of holiness, teach me your ways of gentleness and strength. Hear my humble prayer offered with heartfelt confidence to beg this favor (mention your intention here).

Day 2: O Mary, conceived without sin, I come to your throne of grace to share the fervent devotion of your faithful Mexican children who call to you under the glorious Aztec title of Guadalupe. Obtain for me a lively faith to do your Son's holy will always: May His will be done on earth as it is in heaven.

Day 3: O Mary, whose Immaculate Heart was pierced by seven swords of grief, help me to walk valiantly amid the sharp thorns strewn across my pathway. Obtain for me the strength to be a true imitator of you. This I ask you, my dear Mother.

Day 4: Dearest Mother of Guadalupe, I beg you for a fortified will to imitate your divine Son's charity, to always seek the good of others in need. Grant me this, I humbly ask of you.

Day 5: O most holy Mother, I beg you to obtain for me pardon of all my sins, abundant graces to serve your Son more faithfully from now on, and lastly, the grace to praise Him with you forever in heaven.

Day 6: Mary, Mother of vocations, multiply priestly vocations and fill the earth with religious houses which will be light and warmth for the world, safety in stormy nights.

Beg your Son to send us many priests and religious. This we ask of you, O Mother.

Day 7: O Lady of Guadalupe, we beg you that parents live a holy life and educate their children in a Christian manner; that children obey and follow the directions of their parents; that all members of the family pray and worship together. This we ask of you, O Mother.

Day 8: With my heart full of the most sincere veneration, I prostrate myself before you, O Mother, to ask you to obtain for me the grace to fulfill the duties of my state in life with faithfulness and constancy.

Day 9: O God, You have been pleased to bestow upon us unceasing favors by having placed us under the special protection of the Most Blessed Virgin Mary. Grant us, your humble servants, who rejoice in honoring her today upon earth, the happiness of seeing her face to face in heaven.

Concluding Prayer (to be said each day)

Our Father

Hail Mary

Glory Be

Pray the novena using the Pray Catholic Novena app:

https://pray.app.link/ourladyofguadalupenovena

Chapter Twenty-Eight: The Stories of Answered Prayer

St. Anthony and Hurricane Harvey

I am new in the Catholic faith and have been blessed so many times with answers from God through St. Anthony. I was in a bible study when his name came up. This interested me and I questioned the group and wanted more explanation. Shortly after this enlightenment were devastated by Hurricane Harvey and were displaced from our home.

Lacking any kind of security in the beginning our forgetfulness took over. The recognition of the little we had left seemed to set in quickly. Through this trial I have been answered so many times immediately as to the location of important things that have seemingly disappeared.

I felt guilty at the beginning asking for assistance of material objects but have come to realize it is not a selfish action to ask for assistance from these higher powers. God is truly listening and also wants us to ask Him. Trust and faith have taught me to ask for this help without feeling guilty.

Our Lady of Knock Returns Child to the Faith

Our Lady of Knock interceded to bring my daughter back to Confession, the Eucharist, and to the Sacrament of Matrimony. She continues to keep my family practicing their faith even if not fully. I believe they will be drawn by her to the fullness of faith over their lifetimes so her intercession is always to be prayed for.

St. Joseph and the Imprisoned Fiance

I have prayed many novenas; one sticks out the most and that is the Novena to Saint Joseph. I have prayed faithfully for my fiancé who now is converting to Catholicism after doing two years of RCIA faithfully. He is now serving in a men's ministry at our church and attends mass every Sunday by my side.

This is a man who grew up without Church in his life, spent time in prison, lost his father (who was the only parent he ever knew, as his mother sadly left him at 6 months old). So yes St Joseph's our patron saint!

54 Day Rosary for House and Community

I was looking for a house in a fantastic small Catholic community that I knew would be a great place to live.

I looked for a very long time, and houses that were at all suitable got snapped up or I got outbid and they were gone.

I prayed constantly, especially after each Sunday when I attended Mass at the church in this community. I so badly wanted to live there. I am a member of the parish and involved in many parish activities. I am also very active with the Knights of Columbus council in the community. It is a small town, and I am a small town kind of guy, so this place feels just right to me.

I offered a few Novenas for this cause as well. Then, I heard about the 54-day Rosary Novena, through the website with Father Richard Heilman and the Holy League. I decided to pray this Novena for our Nation (it ended on the Feast of Our Lady of the Rosary, right before the 100th anniversary of the

Fatima apparitions). I also offered the Rosary Novena for my intention, of finding a home in this community.

It happened on day 9 of the Novena. My realtor sent me an email with the pictures of this house. It looked perfect and the price was doable! I went and looked at it, and everything about the house was just what I needed. I told the realtor... "where do I sign".

Our Lady came through for me. Her intercession is powerful, indeed!

I have lived here for a month now. I am 0.3 miles from church, and so can even walk to Mass. I am now able to attend daily Mass now almost every day, even on workdays, since I get to church so quickly.

It is fantastic. I was beginning to think I would never find a suitable place in this small community. But with God (and especially with the help of the Mother of God) anything is possible.

Blessed Kateri and a New Teaching Career

When I was a child I would set up my dolls and play school. I have wanted to be a teacher that long! Making choices for myself without God caused me much heartbreak as well as damaging others.

By the time I was 42, I had recovered from serious sin and began to learn about Christ through His Church, the one I was baptized into yet knew nothing about. I had 3 children and had completed my 12th year of running a childcare business in my home. I deeply desired to teach and, although I had graduated from college 21 years prior and had only read 6 or 7 trade books to update myself, I thought I would apply directly for a teaching position.

We were on vacation and there was an article about Blessed Kateri. It was the first time I really understood what intercessory prayer to saints was all about and, being unsure whether or not I should pursue a full time job, I requested Blessed Kateri to intercede for me and let me know. Weeks and a few phone calls from schools went by. On July 14th I had an interview late morning at my own hometown school. I went to 8 am mass and discovered it was Blessed Kateri's feast day. What a sign! I was offered a job in that district as well as another, but selected my home town for obvious reasons.

Dog Bark Conversion

Our answer to prayer was from Our Lady, when we were pretty convinced of the Catholic Faith but still wondering about praying the rosary.

A dog across the street was barking night and day. In the evening the dog was still barking. My husband and I were annoyed during the day by the loud barking, but now that we had put our kids to bed we were concerned it would wake our children. Ben said we should try praying to Mary, and if the dog stopped barking, we would start praying the rosary.

He prayed something like, "Mary, if you can hear me, please make the dog stop barking." That dog stopped practically in mid-bark, and we have been asking for Our Lady's intercession ever since.

(Author's note: God used a dog barking to push this family over the finish line to become Catholic and pray the Rosary!)

A Deathbed Conversion

We prayed a novena for three members of our family to return to the faith. Many other members of the family participated and all three became Catholic or are returning to active participation in the faith and are still committed Catholics today.

The interesting part for me, is that the hardest nut to crack was my brother and this is kind of morbid, but it was my mother's death that caused him to return to the faith. My mother prayed that novena with us and around a month later she passed away. My mother was to be the sponsor for her daughter-in-law (whom we included in the prayer) and my soon-to-be brother-in-law, was so moved by the funeral of my mother that he commented about how that singular event really inspired him to join the Catholic Church. He had never witnessed such a beautiful funeral.

And prior to this time, and her death, my mom had never prayed a Novena before. We came to know about Novenas through the Mary Foundation and reading Bud MacFarlane's books (Pierced by a Sword). My brother said that when my Grandmother passed away a couple of years earlier, it almost killed him. But when our mother died, he had a choice - he was either going to return to his faith or die (I don't think he ever considered suicide, but that is how awful he felt at the two losses). He has a very big heart and was very, very close to my mother.

St. Brendan Makes a Surprise Conversion

I like to attribute my conversion to the intercession of St. Brendan, the patron saint of navigators.

As a child, I had an obsession with all things nautical (which remains in many ways to this day.) My dad, who at the time was strongly anti-Catholic, and anti-organized church in general, came across a tiny lapel pin at a local Christian store on their one tiny Catholic display. The pin was a simple oval, depicting St. Brendan behind a sailor at the wheel, with the words, "St. Brendan Pray For Us" imprinted around the frame.

Though my dad and I often clashed, we are rather frighteningly alike and he is very dear to me, and I wore the pin on my jacket or shirt collar religiously on every occasion I had a chance to do so, even super gluing a thumb tack to the back when the original pin broke off (the glue is still holding).

Once, cautious and stammering, certain Protestant friends asked, "um, so...are you...uh...Catholic?"

Stunned, I denied it vehemently, and asked why they would think so, to which the young man replied, "well, I saw your little saint."

It became a running joke thereafter, and developed into a practice of the three of us huddling in a circle and crossing ourselves.

It would be a good many years before I finally found myself being pulled into the irresistible. Now, as the only Catholic in my family, despite having also been the most anti-Catholic among my siblings, I confidently believe that for years I was unknowingly invoking the prayers of a silent but patient witness.

Today, I have taken St. Brendan as my confirmation saint, and he is my little family's self-professed patron to whom my wife and I regularly go for continued intercession, especially for guidance of our family in the will of God and in navigating the oceans of our life.

Trusting God in Trials

"Trust in the Lord with all your heart, and lean not on your own understanding." (Proverbs 3:5) These words are written on a small prayer card given to me by my grandmother when I was young. I read that card many times growing up, but it wasn't until my young adult life that I really started to learn what it meant and how to do it.

Through various trials, the Lord has been showing me a way to a deeper union with Him: trust. Many times God has taken something away from me, only to draw me closer to Him— and often give me something better than what He took. He has called me to trust Him with what He was doing, and be open for what He has next.

At the dawn of our marriage, the Lord put on the hearts of my wife and I the desire to raise much of our own food. The dream was to raise enough money to someday buy a house with enough land to homestead on the

side while teaching theology for my day job.
Two years ago, we came across the New
Catholic Land Movement, and after reading
Kevin Ford's material, I decided to contact him
and compliment him on his work.

Much of what he wrote had spoken to my
wife and I (in fact, we had backed up to the
beginning of his blog in order to read the whole
story). Quickly a friendship developed between
our families, and (long story short) the Fords
invited us to join them on their farm.

This was a big leap for Amanda and me.
We were going to leave a comfortable theology
teaching job in Texas to move to the-middle-
of-nowhere, Kansas, to become co-owners of a

farm (for which neither of us had any experience). Nonetheless, both of us felt God leading us in this direction. All of us had ideas of bringing more families onto the land, and starting an institute for rural Catholic life, where we could pass along not only farming know-how but theology as well (Kevin is also a former theology teacher). This was it: God was giving us our "in" for the agrarian life. Of course, this was all much sooner than we had expected, but with God, I've learned over and over again to just follow His timing, and things will turn out better than I could have ever imagined.

After a year of farming, door after door was closing for getting housing for other

families who wanted to move out with us.
Dreams of an agrarian Catholic cultural revival
in this small town were seeming more and
more distant.

Beyond that, farming was getting
tougher and tougher. On the heels of the worst
drought years on record, we had a spring
drought this year. Summer drought is one
thing, but spring drought is a farm-killer.
Mature plants respond much better to
irrigation in the middle of a drought than seeds
and seedlings–most of which we couldn't even
get into the ground because there was no rain
to soften the soil enough for us to effectively
till. If it weren't for our greenhouses, we

wouldn't have had any spring crops. All of our summer crops were pushed back drastically.

And problems didn't stop there. A literal plague of grasshoppers (numbered in the millions) descended on our farm. This happened last year and wiped out half of our crops. After they died down at the end of last season, we spread grasshopper bait at 10 times the recommended level; we put pigs in some of the areas where they had bred, so they would root up the dirt and eat any grasshopper eggs therein. We also released guinea fowl and ducks on the farm to eat the assaulting insects. Alas, however, they came back worse this year. Not to mention the drastic increase in tomato horn worms and

squash bugs.

All told we will probably lose 80-85% of

our crops this year. Ugh! Because of this, our

farm will not be able to bring in enough income

to support our families through the rest of the

year. We already knew that it would be difficult

because we rely mostly on subscriptions to our

delivery service, and we were only able to sign

up about half the number of patrons we

needed to survive the year. As it is, we are

already going to have a difficulty giving those

few customers enough produce to offset the

money they invested. We started seeing the

writing on the wall about a month ago. Our two

families met for a heart-to-heart discussion,

and we decided to pray about where God is leading each of our families (and whether we should close the farm after this season).

Initially, we were shocked, sad, and really felt bad for our customers invested in us and who rely on us for good food. We also didn't know what we were going to do with the fixer-upper house we bought.

Two things became clear: one family needed to move so the other could try to survive until the end of the year, and the obvious choice was our family because Kevin has family here, and he is a much better/more experienced farmer than me. Questions remained, however: Didn't God bring us here to farm and re-establish a community? Didn't

He provide us with this inexpensive house? How do we sell a house in a village of fewer than 30 people? Didn't my in-laws buy the house next door? What will they do? What will we do for income? Do I return to teaching theology to bring in money and perhaps garden as a hobby? Where do I find a job at this time of year? Halfway through the summer, theology jobs are generally already filled for the next year. What will the Fords do for income? If we leave early, they can last a little longer, but they will need help and a new job, too.

Again, I had to rely on that passage from Proverbs: "Trust in the Lord with all your heart, and lean not on your own understanding." I had to trust God that He brought us to Kansas to farm and that He allowed the natural disasters to occur to push us onto the next step in His plan for us. I could not "lean on my own understanding." I don't have the vision that God has. I could not immediately understand all His motives for allowing what He has allowed. Whatever that plan was, I had to trust that He would make it happen. Thankfully, He has put me through many similar situations (though perhaps not on this scale), so I was a bit prepared. Through this whole ordeal, I've felt like His little lamb from Psalm 23:

"The LORD is my shepherd, I shall not want; he makes me lie down in green pastures. He leads me beside still waters; he restores my soul. He leads me in paths of righteousness for his name's sake. Even though I walk through the valley of the shadow of death, I fear no evil; for thou art with me; thy rod and thy staff, they comfort me. Thou preparest a table before me in the presence of my enemies; thou anointest my head with oil, my cup overflows. Surely goodness and mercy shall follow me all the days of my life; and I shall dwell in the house of the LORD forever."

I've felt God's assurance close by me this whole time, and I knew that I just needed to trust Him.

Knowing that God often wills for us to help each other in completing His will, I also reached out to some close friends and family who I knew would pray for us. Amanda and I began the novena (nine days of prayer) to the Sacred Heart of Jesus and asked them to pray along with us. The very next day, my friend told me that the position he just left (in order to attend grad school) had yet to be filled and that he was going to pass my name along to the pastor.

This position is the Director of Student Outreach at St. Mary University Parish on the Campus of Central Michigan University. The following day, the pastor contacted me. In the past, it has always been a good sign of where God is leading me when an opportunity reaches out to me instead of me gaining something on my own. As my former spiritual

director advised me, "you paddle, and let God

do the steering." In those situations, I have

been forced to be weak (letting God bring the

opportunity to me on His own terms and

timing) rather than strong (me aggressively

pursuing the opportunity). I couldn't help but

think of 2 Corinthians 12:9-10:

'but He said to me, "My grace is

sufficient for you, for my power is made

perfect in weakness." I will all the more gladly

boast of my weaknesses, that the power of

Christ may rest upon me. For the sake of

Christ, then, I am content with weaknesses,

insults, hardships, persecutions, and

calamities; for when I am weak, then I am strong.'

Then weak I must be–and be it gladly–for I must realize that whatever God has for me is better than anything I can bring about on my own. Further I dove into my times of prayer, beseeching God for His guidance and clarity (for both me and the parish). If this opportunity panned out, I would be able to fulfill my passion of imparting the faith to young adults (how I got started in ministry/theology back in 2001). Also, I would only be 2 hours from my hometown, with many friends/family (including my best man) within an hour. We would also only be 5 hours from most of Amanda's family.

Up to now, we have never (in our married life) lived less than 6 hours from any family. Through all the places God had brought us, I had always pined for the beauty of Michigan. After having spent the first 31 years of my life in Michigan, I haven't stepped foot on the sandy shores of a Michigan beach. After spending so many of my summer days swimming in Michigan's clear, sand-bottom lakes and bays, I have rarely swam in the dirty muck-bottom waters of Iowa, Texas, and Kansas. It would be a dream come true to return to my native land, and to be able to teach my kids to swim in those same waters where I learned. But would it be?

Trust, I must, and wait. Ah! So many of God's plans involve us waiting, being more and more patient, continually offering up the sacrifice of not knowing and not being able to actively do anything but pray. As the novena went on, we had multiple contacts with the pastor. Then on the Solemnity of the Sacred Heart of Jesus, he called me and set at ease some of our concerns about how much I could earn—ministry jobs aren't known for their ability to provide the single income for a family, but he was able to make it work. He also, in that same conversation, offered to "move things to the next step:" an interview via Skype with multiple members of the parish. There was just one hitch: we had to wait two more weeks for one of them to return from vacation. Again, we were back to being refined in the fires of waiting to form the virtue of patience.

This time was not without its own highlights, though. During the novena, our next door neighbor, Aaron, had heard that we were going to move, so he walked over and offered to buy our house. Not only that, but since he's a carpenter, he offered to buy it "as is," and he will finish our work, meaning we could stop and focus on more important things. We are still waiting to find out what will happen for my in-laws and their fixer-upper house next door, but I'm sure God has a plan for that, too.

Prayer works, I'm telling you! "Pray, hope, and don't worry!" – St. Pio

But wait, there's more: I wrote to an acquaintance I had met through Jeremy, who is a member of the parish. I wanted to know if he knew anything about housing in the area. He responded, and get this: not only does he go to the parish, but the pastor asked him to be on the interview committee, and he happens to own a duplex that might just come up for rent right when we need a place. Not only that, but the other side of the duplex is going to be rented to missionaries with whom I will be working! Yes, God provides:

"Therefore I tell you, do not be anxious about your life, what you shall eat or what you shall drink, nor about your body, what you shall put on. Is not life more than food, and the body more than clothing? Look at the birds of the air: they neither sow nor reap nor gather into barns, and yet your heavenly Father feeds them. Are you not of more value than they? And which of you by being anxious can add one cubit to his span of life? And why are you anxious about clothing? Consider the lilies of the field, how they grow; they neither toil nor spin; yet I tell you, even Solomon in all his glory was not arrayed like one of these. But if God so clothes the grass of the field, which today is alive and tomorrow is thrown into the oven, will he not much more clothe you, O men of little faith? Therefore do not be anxious, saying, 'What shall we eat?' or 'What shall we drink?' or 'What shall we wear?' For the Gentiles seek all these things; and your heavenly Father knows that you need them all. But seek first his kingdom and his righteousness, and all these things shall be yours as well. "Therefore do not be anxious about tomorrow, for tomorrow will be anxious for itself. Let the day's own trouble be sufficient for the day. (Matthew 6:25-34)

No wait, there's still more: A few days later, we found out that Amanda is pregnant! So, counting our little Simon Peter (in Heaven) and Miriam Ruth (on Earth), we have Baby #3 due March 3rd! We again deepened our

prayers.

Amanda came across another novena

that was coming up: that to Our Lady of Mount

Carmel. Both Amanda and I wear the Brown

Scapular as a sign of our devotion to Jesus

through Mary, who gave the scapular to St.

Simon Stock on Mount Carmel July 16th 1251,

so this is a prominent Memorial for both of us.

We don't normally pray back-to-back novenas,

but this time it seemed appropriate. We prayed

both to get the job and for the health of the

baby (having lost Simon Peter, we're

particularly sensitive to baby health).

Today, on the Memorial of Our Lady of

Mount Carmel, we were supposed to have that

interview. On Monday, however, the pastor called me, asking to move the interview up a day. I couldn't help but wonder, what if Our Lady is praying so that things move up and we will be offered the job on her memorial? Well, that is just what happened! Praise God, the interview went well, and they decided to hire me!

So let's recap: God took away the farm, only to bring me: 1) a new job, returning to my passion of teaching theology to one of my favorite age groups, 2) a return to my beloved state of Michigan, 3) a buyer for my house, 4) a potential place to live, and 5) a new baby. God is so good!

I encourage you, if you are in any trial now (or in the future): place your trust in Him. Yes, I know it's scary. I know you'll probably have to let go of something(s), but He has a plan for you. Yes, He has a plan for you–not just me or some other guy: *you*. He wants to give you something even better for you (that which will draw you closer to Him and will draw other souls closer to Him through you), if you let Him. The question is: "Are you going to lean on your own understanding, or are you going to trust Him?"

Always trying to trust more and more!

(Author's note: This story was sent to me from my friend Casey and appears originally on his site here:

https://caseyltruelove.wordpress.com/2014/07/17/trusting-god/)

Masters Degree Saved!

I prayed several novenas for this intention, and many of my family members and priest friends were praying too, and offering masses. At the end of the day, prayer worked, even when there seemed no way out.

This happened while I was pursuing my Masters degree in electrical engineering. Just a month before my dissertation, things happened that were beyond my control that derailed my project work. I was stressed and didn't see how I would finish on time. But I kept praying, as did my entire family. Through your app, I've prayed several novenas - to St. Jude, St.

Joseph, The Sacred Heart, Mother Mary and others.

Praise be to God that by no strength of my own, my presentation went on smoothly. I even got a full score even though my system didn't meet all the target specifications! All this is only because of God's grace and not any of my abilities. Prayer indeed does work and miracles do happen!

Once again, thank you for building the pray app.

Police and Cancer

In late medieval Christianity, Michael, together with Saint George, became the patron saint of chivalry and is now also considered the patron saint of police officers, paramedics, firefighters and the military, and so my story begins.

I entered Law Enforcement in my late twenties at a time when women were making their presence known as police officers. I was baptized Catholic and was taught my prayers by my foster grandparent, who every night would have the other children in the house sit before him and recite the traditional Catholic prayers, "Our Father" Hail Mary etc., before going to bed. I have had a special devotion to the Holy Mother since then, always calling out to her and Jesus, especially when I would get earaches.

One night, my ears were hurting and my foster grandmother tried her home remedy of rolling up a newspaper into the shape of a cone, inserting the point of the cone into the ear, while lighting the other end of the cone, hoping that the heat would draw out the wax from the ear, hence, ease the pain. When that did not work, I was sent to bed to deal with the pain until I fell asleep.

As I lay in a fetal position and whimpering, praying the Hail Mary, asking her to take this pain from me, I fell into a deep sleep. Suddenly I began to feel my body floating upward. I was almost to the ceiling and looked down and saw my body style lying in bed while going up through the ceiling and out into the night, going higher and higher into the night sky. Suddenly I saw on both sides of me Angels. They were so beautiful and then suddenly I saw a beautiful light and I heard a woman's voice that was unlike I had ever heard, so beautiful.

I heard her say, "Take her back; it is not her time". I yelled "No", I want to go with you, please take me! Soon I was falling away from this beautiful voice and down back into my room and into my bed. When I woke the next morning, my earache was gone and to this day I have never had another earache.

As a result my faith grew stronger and my prayer life more intense from that day. I began to not only pray more faithfully, but learned more about the Saints within my Catholic faith. I wanted to know more of the power of the Novenas and soon it became part of my prayer life, as I would call upon two special Saints over the next 10 years.

One night while on patrol working the graveyard shift, I was headed back to the station when a car flew past my unit, running a red light at an intersection. As I pursued the car onto the freeway, I began to pray to St. Michael, (underneath my vest was the St. Michael medal I wore). As the vehicle pulled over just by the on-ramp, I noticed the movement in the car by the passenger and the driver, and for a moment I lost sight of him.

Praying to St, Michael, I exited my unit, and a strange feeling came over me. It was though someone was near me, but there was no one there. I moved to the back of my unit while waiting for the follow-up to arrive, something inside my thoughts just said, "do not approach the car".

When I was finally able to approach the car and we were back at the station, and had in custody both the driver and the passenger, it was discovered that the driver had a loaded .38 caliber gun up to his chest when I pulled him over and he was going to shoot whoever came up to the car.

I gave thanks that night going home to my daughter to St. Michael for his protection and answering my prayers. I always made sure I wore my medal.

In 2001 I was diagnosed with an aggressive Non-Hodgkin's Lymphoma, which started, in my spleen. St. Peregrine is the patron saint of cancer patients. I had always told God that His will be done, not mine, so when I was diagnosed, I only wanted to pray and do all that I could to follow the help of the doctors whom

God placed in my path to treat me.

God is the ultimate healer but gives us those whom he has given as healers here on earth. The saints are there to be our intercessor in time of need so that we can all upon them and believe that God grace is through them.

St. Peregrine, like St. Paul, was in open defiance of the Church as a youth. Once given the grace of conversion he became one of the great saints of his time. He was cured of cancer, after he received a vision of Christ on the cross reaching out his hand to touch his impaired limb, with a cancerous growth. It became so painful he sought amputation and the night before the surgery, Peregrine spent hours in prayer, upon dozing off and going into a dream that Christ was touching him and

healing his foot. He had been completely
healed.

There is a mission in San Juan
Capistrano where the statue of St. Peregrine is
and so I would go as often as I could there to
pray, asking for his intersession for my own
cancer. I believe my prayers and novena's to
him were answered, in that although there is
never a cure for cancer, I have been in
remission since.

I love my Catholic faith for several
reasons, but most importantly the gifts of the
Sacraments, the Saints and The Holy
Eucharist.

Novena Didn't Work

God has answered many prayers for me. But...yes, there is a but. I desperately want and have prayed for a promotion at work. I have prayed numerous novenas, lit candles, had others pray for me. And... nothing. This has been going on for a year. I'm sad, frustrated, desperate, you name it. It feels that it will never happen for me. Where do I turn?

Author responds: This kind of situation is very hard. What I have seen in my life in such situations is: what I thought would be the solution for me (e.g. new position or a promotion at work) later on was not what I needed at all, and instead God brought a different plan for me entirely (meeting someone, a big move, a change in perspective), and that the struggle itself was important in me looking for a new position or promotion as I learned many things that helped me discover the real thing God was leading me to.

God is the master weaver of all the threads in our lives and across lives. That said, it can be very difficult when you are a hard time to know what will come next or what you should do.

Healed ACL for World Youth Day

Just last year I had torn my ACL (the most crucial ligament running vertically through the knee). Having torn it I couldn't walk without the assistance of crutches.

Later, I found out that I had completely torn the ligament, needing a surgical operation to fix it. The surgery would take me away from my vital school work, my family, and leave me in a hospital. Furthermore, I was just going to World Youth Day in a couple of days so I was really feeling down on my luck.

Also my mum and dad could not afford a surgery. So the only thing I knew to do was to pray. I prayed The Novena to Our Lady of Fatima to cure my leg. And by the end of the

9th day I could walk without the assistance of my brace. My leg was in a remarkably stable condition from having completely torn it.

Miraculously, it was healed enough to go to World Youth Day. At first, the chance of me being able to get around without a wheel chair were looking very slim, but after praying the novena I was healed enough to walk properly.

The kicker? When I came back home from World Youth Day I didn't even need the surgery. It had healed itself miraculously.

Healing and St. Therese

Although God has answered a number of my prayers over the years through the intercession of a saint, most often Saint Anthony for lost items, there is one time in particular that stands out for me.

My father was in the hospital after many years of struggling with the disease of emphysema. His heart failed during the night and the doctors had to resuscitate him and place him on a breathing machine.

I turned to Saint Therese the Little Flower in a novena for nine days asking her intercession with the Lord to allow my father to live and spend more time with his wife and ten children here on earth. We were not ready to let him go. Shortly after the end of the nine day novena, I was startled to see a

magnificent rose cover the screen of the TV
that had been on while I was getting ready for
work. I was not watching the TV and just
happened to glance at the screen the moment
the rose appeared.

I had no idea what TV program was
airing at the time and why it featured this
beautiful flower. I later thought that perhaps it
was a feature about the upcoming flower show.
That's a possibility.

But, moments after seeing the rose, I
knew St. Therese was telling me that God
would answer my prayers. I was elated. My
father would recover and return home to his
loving wife and children. This blessing gave my

family time to prepare for the eventual death of my father a little more than a year later.

My family is so grateful to have had such a wonderful earthly father and for our loving and compassionate heavenly Father.

The Job Came Through

God has answered our prayers. My husband had been unemployed for a long time. He had gotten a few small jobs and just this past month, a miracle occurred. He interviewed for a firm and is now employed back in his field of work.

We are so thankful that our prayers were answered. Have faith in God, He knows what you need and will answer you.

We prayed to Our Lord Jesus and the Blessed Mother, along with St. Jude, and St, Francis. I know that they were all listening and sent this miracle to us!

St. Rita and Blindness

Two years ago just out of the blue my then 8 year old son started to lose his sight. According to him everything was just blurry. He stopped going to school. It was a very sad and stressful time ... I mean one moment he was fine the next moment he couldn't see a thing, no sickness, no accident. We took him to different doctors and specialists, and all the doctors we saw couldn't find anything wrong with his eyes or eyesight.

Then my mum who's a devout Catholic suggested we pray the St. Rita novena plus fasting. So my mother, sister, and I started the novena and fasting and before we even finished the novena my son gained his sight back. One morning during the course of the novena when I had just finished praying the novena prayers that day, I had just come from dropping off my other 2 kids at school and my son who had lost his sight was lying in his bed suddenly came into my room without bumping into anything and he said to me "Mum please take me to school I can see now clearly."

I was confused. I asked him are you sure? He said yes Mum. I asked to walk around the house to see if indeed he was able to see and he did without bumping into things, without having to hold on to the walls while walking. I was so overjoyed God had answered my prayers.

I quickly took him to school, he was late but he was excited, his teachers couldn't believe.

We then turned our asking novena to thanksgiving.

So yes God answered my prayers and I'm so grateful. My son is 10 now and the best in his class how can I not thank God? To Him be all the glory!

Chapter Twenty-Nine: Godspeed Your Way to Heaven through Prayer

We've all had prayers that have not been answered the way we hoped. Mixed with the clear affirmative answers to prayer are those frequent times when things didn't go as desired. Does this disprove God's existence, or His caring for us? Absolutely not. Rather, it demonstrates that He knows better than we do what will actually be best for us. If it were up to me, I'd choose a life of ease, comfort, and security. But that is not necessarily what will make me a saint.

What is remarkable is that, as the preceding stories show, sometimes what we pray for does align with God's perfect will for us, and we see the astounding, amazing, even miraculous fruits of that prayer. God certainly uses these experiences to confirm our faith in Him, and to witness to others.

Now that you have finished this book, what next step could you take to deepen your prayer life? I suggest taking the next step and begin to learn mental prayer. Vocal prayer is the first level of prayer; the second level is mental prayer, also called Catholic meditation. This kind of meditation is the true kind, not an Eastern mysticism, not an emptying of oneself of all desire, but rather a filling of oneself with God. St. Alphonsus Liguori said that every saint became a saint, through mental prayer.

You have probably already done mental prayer before, even without knowing it. It is a time where you turn your heart to God in silence: a simple interior gaze at Jesus, a contemplation of His beauty, omnipotence, omniscience, infinite care, mercy, and graciousness. You then let Him touch your heart and mind, sometimes with your imagination and memory active, sometimes with them still. This reflection on God leads to a response, sometimes called affections, which could include sorrow for sin, gratitude to Him, a conviction to lead a better life, to conquer a habitual vice, and so on. This in turns leads to petitions for the needs of yourself and others that come to your mind, and finally to a resolution to amend your life in a concrete way.

I recommend seeking out books and presentations on meditation. Ones that reference the saints are best, or that come recommended from the treasury of the Church.

Thank you again for praying and seeking our Lord, and be assured of my prayers. I am,

Yours Truly,

Devin Rose

Feast of St. Justin Martyr

Other Books by Devin Rose:

- The Protestant's Dilemma:

  https://shop.catholic.com/the-

  protestants-dilemma-how-the-

  reformations-shocking-consequences-

  point-to-the-truth-of-catholicism/

- Navigating the Tiber:

  https://shop.catholic.com/navigating-

  the-tiber-how-to-help-your-friends-and-

  family-journey-towards-the-catholic-

  faith/

Printed in Germany
by Amazon Distribution
GmbH, Leipzig

30898059R00189